WILL WE EVER MEET AGAIN?

WILL WE EVER MEET AGAIN?

A Bridge between this World and the Next

Tom Colton

MERCIER PRESS
Cork
www.mercierpress.ie

ISBN: 978 1 78117 247 6

10 9 8 7 6 5 4 3 2 1

A CIP record for this title is available from the British Library

Printed and bound in the EU.

Tom Colton is one of the most intriguing radio interviewees we have ever had on the show. The listener interaction is incredible, and he keeps them glued to the radio whilst he accurately connects with their loved ones who have passed on. We could never give his guest-spot enough time!

Niall Boylan, 4FM

~

Details of my uncle Laurence's life, death, family, and messages to both my father and other family members were uncannily accurate. Of course, a sceptic would argue deduction is the key to any psychic reading. But deduction alone can't pinpoint names, dates and cause of death, number of brothers, occupation, favourite tipple and other little idiosyncrasies …

Conor O'Neill, *Belfast Telegraph*

~

Tom Colton is the real McCoy when it comes to mediumship and communicating with the spirits of people who have died. I have seen him at work, and the people he has helped walk away relieved and reassured. People walk away from a reading with Tom truly believing in an afterlife, once he has passed on accurate information and details about their deceased loved ones that only they would know. I have seen him come up with names, hair colour, times and places of death, and many other precise details about people who have died that he never met or knew of before. He is spreading a message too – that there is more to life than our current existence; that when we stop breathing, souls inside us live on – and I like that message. Ireland has seen an explosion of interest in spirituality and mediumship in recent years and I believe Tom is one of the genuine good and honest mediums out there.

Kevin Jenkinson, *Irish Daily Star*

DEDICATION

> When someone you love becomes a memory, that memory becomes a treasure.
>
> *Author unknown*

This book is dedicated to my dear uncle, Richard Kealy, who died of leukaemia in 2001. It was because of his passing that I got back onto my spiritual path, and this was instrumental to me developing my mediumship ability.

CONTENTS

ACKNOWLEDGEMENTS

To my wife Linda, with thanks for your support. To my children, Ben, Katie, Darragh and baby Charleigh, born on New Year's Day 2012 at 1.27 a.m. – the second baby to be born in 2012 in Holles Street Hospital, Dublin – I love you all dearly.

To my mother Ann, who gave birth to me at twenty-eight weeks, and my father Tom, whom I respect and love dearly, thank you both for your love, support and encouragement. Thanks also to my brother Anthony and sisters Anita and Natalie.

To all who have helped me on my path, and those who have taught me life lessons – the nice ones and the hard ones – I thank you.

I also have to thank all of the staff and management of the Delphi Mountain Resort (www.delphimountainresort.com) in Connemara, Galway. I spent eight nights there while writing some of this book. Situated in one of the most beautiful places in Ireland, with a backdrop of mountains, lakes and forests, the resort provided me with a haven of peace, tranquillity and stillness to get the book finished. No TV, no mobile-phone signal – just the stillness and peace nature has to offer. Pure bliss! I definitely will be back there to do the second book!

To all of those who contributed to the book: my colleagues, Julie Simpson, Robert Wright, Orla Shevlin, Irene 'Durham' Simpson, Lurleen Drumm, Christine Noctor, Melissa Bruce and Marie S., and all of those who shared their experiences and stories, thank you on behalf of Spirit. To all the team at the Spiritualist Union of Ireland, for all their hard work and dedication to Spirit – especially Mary Losty and John Fitzgerald.

To Bernie, who has supported me and has been there for me since I became a full-time medium in 2009, thank you.

To my amazing agent, Susan Feldstein, for all her hard work and dedication, thank you – you will be rewarded in the Spirit World for all your efforts! To all the team at Mercier Press – true professionals at what they do – for all their hard work and dedication to the book, I thank them.

And last but not least, to those in the Spirit World who have provided me with their support, wisdom, messages and encouragement – without these, I would just be a mad man talking to myself. I am indebted to you all, my Spirit friends.

Tom

www.tomcolton.com

Encouraging the Spirit, Enlightening the Heart

INTRODUCTION

The purpose of this book is to tell my story as a medium, share my experiences and some of the readings that I have done (where a person comes to a medium to communicate with a loved one who has passed), and to let people know that we all have the ability to communicate with Spirit.[1] A key message of this book is that there is no special gift involved – it is an ability we all have the potential to develop.

All of those I deal with in my role as a medium have one

1 Throughout this book, I use the term 'Spirit' to refer to a number of different things. 'Spirit' or 'Spirit person' may refer to the individual spirit of someone who is no longer on this earth plane. 'Spirit' may also refer to the Spirit World or Realm, which is in another dimension to our life on this earth. 'Spirit' may also denote the Divine or Creative Energy in which I and all Spiritualists believe: an indestructible force which has created all there is. It is my belief that energy cannot be destroyed; it can only change form. Thus while, after death, the physical body is left behind, the soul (Spirit) continues to exist in the Spirit World. The individual personality continues unchanged by the event we call 'death'.

key thing in common – the experience of bereavement. Such a simple word, yet one that encompasses so much. If you have ever been bereaved, you will have some familiarity with the feelings of anxiety, sometimes anger and all the other varied emotions that it can arouse. It is unfortunate that often those people who are helping us through our bereavement have not actually experienced it themselves and hence do not understand the unknown vastness into which we have been plunged.

When a loved one dies (crosses over), we often start to question our relationship with the person who has crossed over. 'What could I have done?' we ask ourselves a thousand times a day. 'What if?' We long just to be able to hold them one more time, to be able to tell them how much we really do care, how much we love them. It does get easier to cope with in time – sometimes a lot of time – yet the feeling of loss never goes away. The truth, however, is that our loved ones never go away either: they are always in our hearts and they are still around us. As someone's Spirit loved one told me one day during a reading: 'I haven't gone anywhere – I have just moved on.'

A medium can help someone who has suffered bereavement with the healing process. Visiting a medium is not a substitute for counselling – it is complementary to it. There is no particular time you have to wait before you can consult a medium, nor is there a limit to the number of times you can visit one. Some people say you have to let your loved ones in Spirit rest for three months, and that you should have your readings six months apart, but this is not so. You should visit a medium when you feel it is right for you, plain and simple. And the truth of it is that you don't need a medium to communicate with Spirit – you can do this yourself, once you know how.

People who have come to me for readings or have attended one of my events get to experience first-hand what it is like to connect with Spirit and feel the presence of a Spirit loved one's energy. Some say it is the most incredible experience they have ever had.

There are, of course, those who do not believe that we humans have the ability to connect with those who have passed on to the Spirit World. Yet how can any individual say that another person is not communicating with Spirit? When a person looks at something with their own eyes, they use their own understanding to perceive what is there and what they see is not necessarily what another would see.

In this book, along with me, others have shared their personal experiences and spiritual journeys, all of which help to affirm the message of this book: that we can all communicate with Spirit in our own way.

1

SO WHAT'S IT ALL ABOUT?

> To fear death, gentlemen, is no other than to think oneself wise when one is not, to think one knows what one does not know. No one knows whether death may not be the greatest of all blessings for a man, yet men fear it as if they knew that it is the greatest of evils. And surely it is the most blameworthy ignorance to believe that one knows what one does not know.
>
> *Socrates*

Put in the simplest way, a Spiritualist medium is someone who can communicate with the spirits of people who have passed away. The purpose of this communication is to relay messages from those who are no longer in this life to loved ones who are still alive. Mediums are the conduit through which the living can make contact with the dead, and vice versa.

In many ways death can be compared to a journey to a faraway country. If you were to take a trip to a foreign land, or move away from those you love, what would be the first thing you would want to do once you arrive at your destination? Most of us would want to call home and let our loved ones know that we got there safely. Thus it is, I believe, when we die. Spirits who have passed from this life to the next simply wish to convey to us that they have completed the journey and are okay. Mediumship is the means through which this communication can take place.

Throughout this book, I make reference to a 'sitter' and a 'communicator'. The sitter is the person who comes for a reading with a medium on a one-to-one basis, or who gets a reading at a demonstration of mediumship. The communicator is the Spirit person who seeks to make contact with their loved one, to give evidence that they still exist: that after the physical body passes, the Spirit body lives on. The medium is the link between the sitter and the communicator. The communicator gives the medium the information and the medium passes this message on to the sitter. To use a very simple analogy, the medium is like a two-way radio to the Spirit World.

Generally speaking, a medium is someone who has

developed their spiritual knowledge and attunement faculties, and has learned how to use these to connect with the Spirit World. But it should be remembered that everyone has the ability to be a medium of some kind. Connecting with the Spirit World is an ability, not a gift only conferred on a privileged few. However, as with any ability, developing one's mediumship to its highest level involves a lot of dedication, hard work and study.

Many people have had some experience of Spirit in everyday life. It's not something that is talked about openly or dwelt on very much by a lot of people – perhaps because there is a certain level of fear of ridicule around such things, as they are not fully understood. In researching this book, I asked a range of different people to tell me about their earliest recollections of 'out-of-the-ordinary' experiences – if they had any – including how they felt at the time and whether they were afraid or otherwise. A large proportion were able to confirm that, yes, they had had such experiences, often from very early on in their lives. Here are some of the replies I received:

> When I was about four or five, it just seemed normal. I saw a little boy upstairs and kept asking my mum who he was. Mum brushed it off but, kindly, didn't discount it.

Years later she told me my aunt had seen him too and had described him in exactly the same way as I had.

~

When I was five or so, I was aware of spirits around me. No, it did not scare me – spirits have never ever scared me. I had lots of minor experiences when I was young; then, when I was about fifteen, I saw my nan, who had died, at the end of my bed with a man I did not know. So I went and told my mum and dad, and they said it was my mum's dad, who I had never met. I was not scared, and my parents believed me.

~

I have had lots of experiences over time and I can't ever remember being frightened. After [it happens,] I am always aware that something that is not of our dimension has taken place. It is a feeling like no other.

~

I never really encountered a spirit on my own, until my first-born came along. When she was two years old we lived alone in a little apartment and I couldn't find her shoes. More to myself than to her, I said, 'Now, Dreamer, where did we put your shoes?' and she replied, 'Dave likes them.' I did and do not know anyone named Dave, by the way. My daughter then kept saying, 'Up!' and I looked up and there were her shoes on top of the fridge, where I'd never put them! And she would constantly babble incoherently to someone who wasn't there.

~

When my mother passed, my youngest ran to our back door which is dead-bolted and never opened, screaming, 'Nanny, Nanny!' The door came open and she stood there crying, reaching up for someone who wasn't there … Also we had set out pictures of my grandparents and parents as a sort of memorial, and my son said to me, 'Who is that?' and I said, 'My papa and he's been in heaven a long time.' My son then became upset and said that I was lying. When I said I never would, he said to me, 'Well, then, who is that guy who follows you all the time?'

~

When I was four or five years old, they [Spirit people] frightened the living daylights out of me. They used to come out of the wall at the bottom of my bed – where there was a fireplace – and stand there, looking at me. Years later, I was told that that actual spot was a portal.

~

> I think that I have felt Spirit from a young age – it was something I could not quite define. There was often a feeling of someone else being around, even when I was alone. In recent years I found out that I had a brother who died at birth, a few years before I was born. I sometimes wonder if it is his spirit that I [have been] feeling but not quite understanding, until recently. No, I don't feel frightened, in fact I feel comforted.

~

> The first time this happened to me, I was about eight. It scared me because I didn't understand what was happening, or who these people were. I welcome my visits now from lost family and friends, and sometimes strangers. I find it very exciting and know how special it actually is.

So it would seem that many people have had encounters with Spirit, but they do not tend to talk about these happenings very much.

In my experience, the public's perception of mediums, fortune-tellers, psychics, tarot-card readers and angel-card readers is that they are all pretty much the same thing. This isn't the case, of course – there are many important differences between these categories. I find that the two figures people most commonly mix up are mediums and psychics, when in many ways they are in fact worlds apart. A medium is someone who connects with a loved one who has passed and delivers evidence of their continued existence in the Spirit World. A psychic is essentially someone who makes predictions about the future. A medium is able to make contact with someone in the Spirit World directly, without the use of any tools, whereas most psychics will work with tools such as cards, rune stones, crystal balls, tea leaves, or by reading the sitter's palm, and so on.

Sometimes I am asked by a client to move into the psychic area. I'm not, however, a fan of doing predictions – I much prefer mediumship, which is where all my instincts lie. My belief in any case is that a Spirit loved one will rarely give information about events and happenings in the future – they will only talk about the past and the here and now. In my view this is because the Spirit World cannot interfere with our life paths. Spirit loved ones will not intervene to alter your course, or give information that may cause you to change someone else's life path. This ties in with my belief that our life journeys are already mapped out by ourselves before we are born and cannot be changed: nothing in this earthly life is coincidental.

Before we come on this earth, each one of us will sign up to our own sacred contract which determines the lessons we will learn in this life.

However, sometimes people will come to me looking not for guidance or a sounding board, but in the hope that Spirit loved ones will intervene and make decisions for them about the future. I remember clearly, for instance, a lady who came for a one-to-one reading, hoping that I could make contact with her brother, who had recently passed. Her brother did indeed come through that day and I began to pass on information from him to my sitter.

'One of the reasons I am here,' this lady then confessed, 'is that I found my partner cheating and I want to know if I should marry him.'

'I am not the person to tell you to marry him or not to marry him,' I replied. 'This is a decision only you – and you alone – can make.'

'Can you ask my brother?' she insisted.

'I will. I know your brother cannot answer this question, but I will ask him anyway.'

When I did so, her brother came through clearly again, with a simple message for his sister: 'You know my feeling on this guy – I have told you already.'

At this, my client started crying. 'I remember very well

the date and the time he spoke to me about this, and what he said to me about my partner: not to trust him!'

'Well,' I replied, 'he is just bringing back that memory to you now, to remind you of his words and how he felt about your partner then,' I said. 'But your brother cannot tell you what to do.'

I believe that Spirit acts in the same way as a good parent would, albeit at a different level of course. Spirit guides don't tell us, they nourish; they don't force, they encourage; they don't push, they support. They will never impose a point of view on us: they will simply pass on their own experiences and impart what they have learned – and it is up to us to take our own philosophy from this.

There are a number of different types of mediumship, most of which fall into one of two broad categories: physical or mental mediumship. Physical mediumship, as its name suggests, involves Spirit communicating via certain physical phenomena, such as noises, voices, objects moving and so on – these are perceptible to everyone present and not just to the medium through whom the connection is being made. Other forms of physical mediumship include 'manifestation' (where a spirit actually becomes visible) and 'direct voice' (where a spirit uses a medium's voice box to communicate directly).

The type of mediumship which I practise falls into the second category – mental mediumship, whereby Spirit communication takes place via the mind or mental processes of the medium, and may only be experienced by that medium: he or she must then interpret and communicate the message to the sitter(s) in attendance.

Within the field of mental mediumship, there are a number of ways in which you can operate – mine is through 'evidential mediumship', which has been described as the best kind of Spirit communication for people with scepticism. This is because in the initial stages of the connection, much of the medium's focus is on bringing through 'evidential' messages from the Spirit loved one – information which proves to the sitter that it is indeed their loved one who is talking to them, by including the type of detail which only they could provide. These are the kind of details of which people will say after a reading: 'The medium knew things about X, my loved one, that they could never have known without being in direct contact with X.'

The exact nature of this evidential detail can vary greatly from reading to reading – and from medium to medium – but the main purpose is always the same: to give information to the sitter that indicates that the connection is genuine and can relate only to their Spirit loved one, and that they can verify as accurate. Some information may require verification after the reading: the sitter may need to consult with friends or other family members who are likely to be privy to the details which have been given. Beyond an immediate message to an individual sitter, evidential mediumship provides proof in a wider sense of the truth of eternal life and the fact that as human beings, we live on in some sense after our physical death.

Here are some examples, from my own experience and that of other mediums I have talked to, of the kind of detail a spirit might provide in order to prove their identity and continued existence:

- Sometimes the medium will get very clearly the name or names of the Spirit loved one, sometimes just the initial.
- A spirit's personality traits may come through.
- Many spirits will be willing to show the medium the circumstances in which they passed.
- Often spirits will give important dates of reference which will have meaning for the sitter.
- Other family members may be referred to, sometimes by name.
- A recent event – sometimes just a minor one – in the

current life of the sitter or of other family members may be mentioned, as a means of demonstrating that the Spirit loved one has an awareness of the here and now, and may even have personally witnessed the event in question.

- Past events may be referred to or shown to the medium.
- A spirit may make reference to their favourite flower, book, song or another treasured object from their life or that of the sitter.

In a sense, I suppose the exact nature of the detail that comes through at a reading is not as important as its *level of accuracy*. Obviously, no one can make categorical statements about the type of information that a spirit will bring to the fore. But just think about it for a while: if you were to die and were suddenly given an opportunity – perhaps the only one – to communicate with your earthly loved ones, what do you think you would want to say to them? Would you really want to give them your old address or telephone number? Would you really want to talk about money or romance? Would you not rather wish to convey some sense of who you *really* are: your personality, your likes and dislikes, what motivated you in life, your most treasured memories of times you spent with loved ones while on earth? And would you not prefer to communicate something along the lines of: 'It's really me; I am here with you; I am okay'?

To me, this point highlights an important difference between a medium's way of working and that of a psychic. A psychic can give predictions and pointers for the future. But only a medium – one who has actually connected with the spirit and energy of your loved one – can convey the true essence and soul of that person. It is this ability that can offer the most meaningful comfort to someone who is grieving, as mediumship is about providing evidence that our Spirit body lives on after we physically pass.

The information that a spirit chooses to communicate will also depend on the medium through whom they are making the connection. Each individual medium will have their own frames of reference and ways of relating to the Spirit World (and indeed to this world also), and this will colour how they receive the information and how they interpret it. In many ways this is where the genius of Spirit communication lies – in knowing the best way of putting across their message to an individual medium. Later we will look in more depth at how each one of us can tune into our own frames of reference and discover our own preferred ways of relating to Spirit, and discuss how everyone has the potential to develop mediumship abilities.

In all of this, it's important to remember too that Spirit communications do not always have meaning in a literal sense – sometimes symbolism or parallels may be used as a way of getting a message across. A favourite story of mine, which illustrates this point well, happened one evening at my development circle (people who come together to learn how to connect and communicate with Spirit) with a lady who had come along for the first time. We always enjoy having new people in the circle, as it gives everyone a chance to connect with a whole different set of Spirit people! On this occasion we were going around the circle in turn, each one of us trying to attune and be receptive to messages from our new member's Spirit loved ones.

When it came to the turn of Barry, one of the regular circle members, he said: 'I can see the film *Annie*, and "Daddy" Warbucks – does this mean something to you?'

'No,' the lady replied. 'Except that I have seen the film.'

At this point, I was able to link in to the communication and I put a question to our sitter: 'Do you understand that your loved one is making reference to a child being given up for adoption?' It was clear to me that the reference that the Spirit World was giving Barry was a symbolic one: alluding to *Annie* was a way of bringing up the subject of adoption, which is of course one of the main themes of that film.

The sitter's jaw dropped, and she looked over at the friend she had brought along with her. 'Yes!' she gasped. 'Not many people know about that, and it's not talked about in the family.' She went on to explain that a child in the family had been given up for adoption many years previously and that they had recently been making attempts to contact this child – who was now an adult, of course – in the hope of rekindling the relationship that had been lost so long ago. It can be seen from this that sometimes a degree of interpretation on the part of the medium and the sitter may be needed in order to fully clarify the message a spirit is trying to put across. Both parties need at all times to be open to the process and attentive to the possible meanings that any one piece of information may hold.

Another example, which further illustrates the extent to which Spirit communication must at times be interpreted rather than taken literally, happened some time ago, again in the context of one of my development circles. On this occasion, in the afternoon of the day of one of our regular weekly sessions, I got a phone call from a girl saying that she was keen to bring her friend along that evening. I said that I would be happy for her to do this and gave her detailed directions about how to get to the venue. A few hours later, however, when I was just about to turn off my phone to start the circle, I got another call. It was the same girl: she told me that unfortunately she had been late finishing work, and that she and her friend were not going to make it along to the circle. But she then insisted that her friend really needed to talk to me and asked if I could possibly ring the friend after I finished my circle. I agreed to do so, although with some reluctance, as I am not a fan of phone or Internet readings.

After the circle session, I rang the friend as promised. She told me she had recently lost someone and asked if I would be able to make contact with them – then and there, on the phone. I explained that I really don't like doing telephone or email readings. I think they are too impersonal and always prefer to be face-to-face with a person, since I am often dealing with a great deal of grief and emotion and so I like to be able to hold the energy of the sitter as well as the energy from the Spirit World. But the girl pleaded with me, saying she really needed to contact her loved one urgently. Realising how important this was to her, I agreed to try for her anyway.

I connected to the Spirit World and asked for loved ones belonging to the sitter to make contact with me. With that, I very quickly felt the energy of a young gentleman connect with me. I was able to describe his appearance:

well dressed, taking pride in the way he looked. I then told my sitter that I had the sensation of falling down the side of what felt like an embankment, banging my head and falling into water, where I had drowned. I next recounted that I was at a canal and that I was there to meet with someone. The girl confirmed that her loved one had gone to meet someone the day he passed. Now I could see the canal area clearly and described the precise location, which the sitter immediately verified.

As I progressed with the reading, the young gentleman said to me in a heavy Dublin accent, 'She's my bird that you are talking to, but she gets thick when I call her that.' So I repeated what he had said.

'He always called me his "bird",' she said, 'and I didn't like it when he said that. I would get annoyed. He would say it sometimes just to wind me up.'

The young gentleman continued, telling me that he had crossed the canal at one of the locks, had lost his footing and fallen into the canal. 'I hate water, I can't even swim,' he said. 'They think I did it meself. But I didn't.' I relayed the information to his girlfriend.

'The gardaí told us he had committed suicide and jumped into the canal himself,' she said. So what I had told her made a lot of sense to her, it seemed. 'He couldn't even swim – he hated the water, so we didn't understand why he would jump into the water in the first place.' Learning now what had really happened was clearly a relief to her.

The reading at this stage had gone on for over an hour. I was completely outside my comfort zone, working over the phone like this – but the information was strong and solid. So I was not expecting the next request from the sitter. After all of the validating evidence that had already come through, she decided she needed to test me further, and said, 'Well, if you really are talking to my fella, ask him to tell you the date we got engaged!'

Well, if that wasn't pressure, what was? One thing I hate is being pressurised when doing a reading, because inevitably the mind kicks in and, rather than just accepting the information as it flows, it starts to try too hard to get the piece of information that the sitter is looking for. Despite this, I said, 'Okay, I will ask.'

Staying calm and trying not to let the tension of the moment get to me, I asked my Spirit communicator the question. With that, he started to laugh, saying to me, 'I'm no April fool!' as he continued to laugh. Now, it was not 1 April or anywhere near it at the time, so I was slightly puzzled and put the question to him again.

He came back with the same reply. 'I'm no April fool!' he repeated insistently, again guffawing with laughter.

Suddenly, I understood. I said to the sitter: 'He keeps saying he's no April fool … He is making reference to 1 April!' There was a thud at the other end of the line, as the girl dropped the phone. Then silence. 'Are you still there? Are you all right?' I started to say. Then I heard the sitter screaming to a friend who obviously was in the room with her: '*He is really there!* He just told me the date we got engaged!' She was sobbing uncontrollably.

Her friend came on the line. I told her to get the sitter to relax, breathe deeply and let herself calm down before she came back to the phone. After a couple of minutes she came back. I asked her if she wanted me to continue. Breathlessly, she said yes, she did. 'That's the date we got engaged! He is really there with you, isn't he? There is no way you could have known that date.'

I connected again with the communicator and asked him for more information around the engagement. He showed me an image of himself making a ring out of a piece of tinfoil. I relayed this to his girlfriend, saying that he was such a romantic, making a ring out of foil, and even going down on one knee to propose – although he had fallen over in the process! The sitter laughed as these details reignited her memories of the event. She said they didn't have the money to buy a ring but that they were going to get one as soon as they could scrape enough cash together. At last she seemed satisfied with what I had been able to tell her and felt able to end the reading there. Relieved and very emotional, this girl had finally been able to put to rest many of the questions that had clearly been torturing her since the death of her fiancé.

From this example, it can be seen that sometimes a key piece of information from Spirit will be relayed in an indirect way, so that the medium or the sitter must be willing and able to interpret what is being said in order to make sense of it.

What also strikes me as a medium about this story is that, despite all the information I had been able to give my sitter throughout the reading, and which she had been able to verify, she still wanted and needed that one detail – the date of their engagement – as a final piece of proof that her boyfriend was indeed communicating with me and that the connection was genuine. This is a very common reaction during readings, I find, and can be more than a little frustrating for a medium. Sometimes people just will not be happy with a communication unless you can tick off all the boxes or manage to obtain a secret code or password from their loved one in the Spirit World. You may have been able to bring through completely accurate information or all sorts of obscure details but, unless you can say one particular word, they won't believe that a connection is real.

The difficulty here from a medium's point of view is that the piece of information that is so crucial to a sitter just doesn't always come to the fore – it is up to the sitter's Spirit loved ones if they wish to engage with providing that one detail in the first place. And, in spite of all my efforts, experience and powers of interpretation, I cannot always understand the sense of certain details that Spirit may be communicating to me. As a medium, I do my utmost to convey all that I feel, hear, see and sense to the person that I read for, but sometimes it is only the sitter who will truly understand – or sometimes not understand, as the case may be.

I always find it really rewarding and encouraging when I give information to someone which they don't feel has any relevance or indeed sense to it, only for them to ring or email a couple of days later to confirm that the information they dismissed had in fact been true and made perfect sense after all. To me, this is the greatest affirmation of Spirit at work. Everything that is communicated in a reading has a purpose, even if we don't understand it at the time. Most importantly, the purpose of a Spirit communication will be to convince the sitter that the realm of Spirit really does exist and that the loved ones they have lost continue to live in a different dimension.

Here is a great illustration of a reading where the sitter was offered very compelling evidence that her loved one in Spirit – in this case her father – continued to exist in the present. In this instance the truth of the information provided could only be established after the event. The sitter's account, in her own words, of what happened is especially powerful:

> I have always believed to some extent that there is life after death. I had been to a few different medium shows in the past, where I have witnessed the joy people got from hearing from their loved ones. I never had the urge to explore it further myself, until my father passed away a few months back. I had heard good reviews from someone who had a reading with Tom and decided to contact him for a reading of my own.
>
> On the day we were to see Tom, I was both excited and nervous. But from the moment we met him, I felt completely relaxed. I had brought a photo of my dad and also his watch to the reading. In what seemed like seconds, Tom had

made a connection with my dad and proceeded to explain exactly how he had passed away. I can't describe the feeling of happiness it gave us, to hear it confirmed, how quick and easy his passing had been. Dad was able to tell us too that his grandmother had been there to help him pass over.

Tom gave so much detail on my father's life and about my family in general that there is just too much to go into (including lots of private things that no one would know besides us), and we were bursting with excitement to tell the rest of the family when we came home.

Just to explain one thing in particular, though. Tom told us that Dad was saying that his chair in the sitting room had been moved – to which we had replied that, no, this wasn't the case. Through Tom, Dad then went on to explain that the chair faced a window and it had been moved. Again we replied no, but we were able to agree that it faced the window. We finished up the reading with Tom passing our father's energy on to us. It was fantastic, to feel the warmth in my chest as I was getting a hug from my dad. I will cherish it forever.

When we arrived home after the reading, I asked my mother if there was anything different about Dad's chair. She told me that the recliner had broken in the other armchair and that because of this, she had swapped it with Dad's. We couldn't believe it! Just goes to show Dad is watching over us and still knows more than us!

> I would recommend a private reading to anybody who has lost a loved one. I believe it is never too soon because it brings you a feeling of peace and a warmth in your heart to hear your loved ones are safe and who they are with.

As a medium, I never claim that I can make a connection 100 per cent of the time, but I will always strive to make contact with specific loved ones in the Spirit World if requested by a sitter and I will always attempt to get that piece of information that only someone close to the Spirit loved one could know.

The messages that come through from the Spirit World never cease to amaze me – in the level of detail that is given, and in the persistence and ingenuity of those seeking to make contact with those on the earth plane. For me, all of this is a powerful confirmation of the central truths which the Spirit World seeks to communicate to us: that our loved ones do survive death; that they go to a place not separated from us by distance, but by dimension. The only things they leave behind, through death, are their physical body and earthly possessions. And, as incredible as these revelations are, there is one even more wonderful still: that we too will survive this mysterious experience we call death.

2

THE MAN CALLED UNCLE

Richard, the man I call uncle, is someone special, to be remembered with warmth, thought of with pride and cherished with love. Richard – you are not only my uncle, but also my friend.

Richard died of leukaemia in January 2001 after a nine-month battle with the disease. His life being taken away from him at the age of thirty-nine was something I couldn't understand at the time. When he died, I asked myself why – why did this exceptional human being have to lose his life at such a young age?

Richard was a trained chef and as a young boy I used to spend time with him some weekends. I wanted to be a chef at the time and would go over to Uncle Richard's house to make cakes, which we would then sell door-to-door in the local area. However, as I grew older, Richard and I had very little contact, even though for about five years we actually lived on the same road. I babysat his two daughters on occasion, but other than that we would barely see each other.

It was not until Richard decided to go into business that I rekindled my relationship with him. I was training to be a chartered accountant at the time and one day he rang me, saying that he was going to start up his own business and wanted me to help him set it up. His idea was to set up a business supplying chefs with equipment and uniforms, and he intended to buy a franchise to sharpen chefs' knives on site at their places of work. So he bought a van, kitted it out with everything he needed and off he went, selling the uniforms and kitchen equipment, and sharpening chefs' knives.

Richard was – and still is – a happy-go-lucky guy, who loves having a laugh. A practical joker, he always has a permanent smile on his face. During his earthbound life, anyone that came into contact with him felt the infectious happiness that this guy radiated. No matter what was happening, my uncle always kept the good side out. On the inside, however, I'd say he was being eaten away as his marriage failed, but his main concern was always the welfare of his two lovely daughters.

Once he had got the equipment and franchise

businesses up and running, Richard's next project was to go about fulfilling a long-held dream, which was to open his own coffee shop. I helped him to realise this dream in 1998. Every night I would read through the property sections of newspapers, and one evening I saw an ad in the *Evening Herald* for business premises for rent on Berkley Road in Dublin. I rang the number that was supplied and got information on the property from the agent. I told Richard of my find – he was so excited at the idea that his dream of opening his own coffee shop was within reach. We both visited the property and met with the then tenant. The premises had been previously used as a small café with about ten tables, but it had a lot of potential. We both knew that our next hurdle would be to raise the finance to get the lease secured and for the initial working capital. But I have never been one to say 'no' to a challenge!

For Richard, however, the timing could probably not have been worse. As his marriage was over, getting a bank loan by remortgaging their house was not an option. But all was not lost. Richard's sister Ann, my mother, was able to lend him the money he needed to start his new venture. The business would be set up in my mother's name, to ensure that all legal aspects of the investment and business operation were correctly administered, but the shop was effectively Richard's and he was going to live his dream.

The previous coffee shop that had been on the site had been called 'Crackpots' and we decided not to change the name, but to add Richard's nickname, which was 'Hacko'. So the shop became Hacko's Crackpots, although we decided to leave the sign above the door as it was for the time being – the change could always be made at a later date. It was agreed that my mother and her sister Pauline would join Richard as part of the team at Crackpots.

Richard was very passionate about food and wanted to offer people a good, nutritious lunch for under IR£5 (approximately €6). All of Richard's food was homemade – soup, quiche, lasagne and so on: absolutely nothing out of a packet. The café soon got a reputation in the area for its quality, low-priced food and soon you had to queue to get a seat in the café at 11 a.m. or lunchtime. People from all walks of life came into the shop – from the guy living on the street to the top surgeons of the Mater Hospital, which was very close by. Richard and his staff treated everyone in exactly the same way, no one was better than the next: everyone was equal.

On one occasion a homeless man came into the café.

With a smile on his face and a clap of his hands, Richard greeted him in the same way as he greeted all his other customers. 'Hi, how's it going? What can I get ya?'

The man replied, 'Son, I don't have any money.'

Richard just said, 'I didn't ask you if you had any money – I asked you what you will have.'

To which the man responded politely, 'I would love a cup of tea and a sandwich.' Richard told him to take a seat and, not long afterwards, he brought down a cup of tea and a sandwich. When the homeless man finished, he came up to the counter, saying, 'God bless you and thank you.'

Every day Richard would walk over to the church on Berkley Road before the 11 a.m. rush, to light a candle and say prayers for anyone who needed it. I met or spoke with him at least once daily, as I was helping him with the finances, tax returns and general operation of the café business. During this time our relationship was not one of uncle and nephew, but more like that of brothers.

Richard continued with his work on the chefs' equipment and uniforms, while also operating the café. In March 2000 he went to his doctor with swollen feet and complaining of continuous tiredness. His doctor referred him to the Mater Hospital for tests and, when the results came back, Richard was diagnosed with leukaemia and given two years to live.

I will never forget the day I heard the news. When I got the phone call, I was in Enniskillen. I started driving home but I hardly knew where I was going. I cried for most of the time as I drove. My head was filled with questions: What do I say to Richard? How can we deal with it, what do I say? As soon as I got home, I went up to his house and he opened the door to me. I simply threw my arms around him, hugging him, and I then started to cry and he cried with me. 'We will get through this,' I said to him. So we sat and chatted about it for a while, as Richard told me about the treatment he was to get and when he had to get it.

Very quickly the knife and equipment franchise was sold off, as Richard was physically and mentally unable to deal with running two businesses while keeping up with his treatments and looking after the girls. In August he was hospitalised. Every day I went to see him on the ward. His progress was not good and Mam said to me that she didn't think Uncle Richard was going to come out of hospital.

My great-grandmother, Anne Carroll, of whom I was very fond, had passed to the Spirit World on 2 August

1988. I was devastated that I didn't get to say goodbye to her, as she passed away on the day I was due to visit her in hospital. 'Granny', as I called her, was very connected to the Spirit World and she had a strong religious faith. Her numerous relics and statues stood tall on the 'altar' in her home – her dressing table. Her favourite saint was Saint Anthony, the patron saint of lost things and missing persons. For as long as I had known her, Granny had been sick with one thing or another. Every Sunday when I used to visit her, she was nearly always in bed, watching Sunday Mass on RTÉ 1. She had a permanent warm smile, and would sit up in the bed, chatting away with me, wearing her glasses with the big rims.

One evening when Richard was in hospital, as I lay on my bed, Granny came to me and I asked her outright: 'Is Richard going to come out of hospital?'

'Yes,' she replied.

It was my first 'real' encounter with Spirit and a communication that I've always remembered. It was as vivid as if I was talking to Granny over a cup of tea in her sitting room on one of those Sunday afternoons when I used to visit her. I told my mother what Granny had told me. But Mam didn't understand, as the doctors had said things weren't looking good at all. Sure enough, however,

Richard did come out of hospital. The doctors decided to put him on a new trial drug, but they warned us that not every patient was reacting well to this drug and that it all depended on the individual.

In December Richard's condition worsened and he was admitted to hospital on the evening of Christmas Day. His prognosis was not good, the doctors told us. His condition had deteriorated significantly and the new drug was not agreeing with him at all. But Richard made the best of the situation. All the time he was in hospital he managed to stay in good spirits, and whenever we went to visit him he would always greet us with his usual smiling face.

One day I got permission from his doctors to take him out of the hospital for half an hour, so that we could walk over to the coffee shop, where we had a surprise in store. We had arranged for the old sign on the shop to be replaced with a new one, on which was the name Hacko's Crackpots. When he saw the sign, Richard smiled broadly – he couldn't believe that his name was finally above the door! We went in and got something to eat, but didn't stay long – he was feeling quite weak, so I brought him back to the hospital reasonably quickly.

Richard stayed in hospital until the week before he passed, when he was taken home and was given hospice care. He did not want to die in hospital, and he was a very strong-willed man. My mother and her sister Pauline cared for him on a full-time basis while the hospice team did their best to make him comfortable, and he was put on a morphine drip. However, even with the amount of medication he was on, on occasion he would get up and walk around the house – much to the amazement of the nurses. 'He shouldn't be able to walk at all, with the amount of drugs he is on,' one of the nurses remarked to us in private.

I will never forget the night Uncle Richard passed. The house was full of his immediate family, including his estranged wife, whom he wanted there. Up until the moment he passed he loved her and idolised the ground she walked on … and he still does.

That evening, Mam, Pauline and I were in the room with Richard, as well as a few others including his wife, who was at the end of the couch. As we sat with him, I fell asleep on one of the chairs, until Pauline woke me up, saying, 'It's time.' In that moment, I suddenly felt as if there was something or someone holding on to my left leg – it was the same sensation as when a child holds on to your leg and is crying because they don't want to leave you. But in this case, there was no one there. It was an unusual feeling – one that I will never forget. My belief is that this was Richard in Spirit, saying that he didn't want to go. (This would be confirmed, many months later, when my sister channelled Richard at one of my development circle meetings. I asked him about that night and if it was him who had held on to my leg, and he confirmed that it was.)

I remember leaving the room, as my aunts and uncles all came in to say goodbye to him. I went into the kitchen, where my girlfriend Linda (now my wife) was sitting with my sister Anita. 'Richard is gone – he is free,' I told them. It was 21 January 2001.

Richard was cremated on 23 January at Glasnevin Crematorium. I knew the staff there, as the cemetery was a client of my accounting firm. I arranged for myself, Mam and her sister Pauline to go there that day to bid Richard's physical self a final farewell. When we arrived, I introduced Mam and Pauline to Mick, who explained what was going to happen next. He looked at the thermostat on the crematory and said, 'I have to wait for the temperature to come down, before I put the coffin in.' We all laughed a little at this, because when Richard was being nursed at home, one of the main things that Mam and Pauline had to work on was keeping his temperature down, with fans and constant cold compresses. I felt this was a sign from my uncle to let us know all was well, and also, as was his way, to add a bit of lightness to the occasion! I can never start talking about Richard and his life without ending up laughing about some story he had told or something funny he had said or done. He was such a bright, positive person, who, as I mentioned, always kept the good side out and had a great sense of fun.

~

In so many ways, Richard's death was a revelation to me – a turning point, after which my life would never be the same. It was my search for answers about how my beloved uncle was after he passed that led me back to my spirituality. I felt such a great need to talk with him – to know how he was and if he was happy – and this drove me to try to discover more about the world of Spirit. The loss of Richard was the catalyst which would bring about a profound transformation in my life, not only on a spiritual level, but also, eventually, in the most concrete way possible, by leading me to undertake an entirely new career.

My mother, Ann, was similarly affected by Richard's passing. Once she was able to recover a little from the first shock of intense grief, a whole new spiritual realm began to open up for her. Before – like so many of us – Mam had been all too aware of the negative things in life. After her brother's death, she would become a much more optimistic and joyful person, and one who dedicated her life to the Angels – and continues to do so. Over the years, I have come to realise that the death of a loved one can be a similarly powerful force for change in many people's lives.

Up until that point in my own life, I had never had any really overwhelming sense of the Spirit World, or if I did, I was not aware of having had any unusual or otherworldly experiences of any kind. Indeed, even once I began to develop my awareness of and ability to connect to the Spirit World, and in fact to this day, I have never felt that there is anything 'other' or out of the ordinary about the way connections take place. I don't enter a different state; I don't hear voices other than my own inner voice; I don't experience Spirit communication as something bizarre or unreal. And it has certainly never felt like something to be afraid of. It all feels perfectly natural to me, and I suppose this tallies with my belief that communication with the Spirit World is something that is open to us all.

~

My introduction to this life was not an easy one. I was born on 15 December 1975 in Dublin's Rotunda Hospital, weighing just two pounds. Just twenty-eight weeks old, I was classed in medical terms as 'extremely premature'. I spent the first months of my life in an incubator and it was six weeks before my mother was allowed to touch, hold or feed me. It was not until 15 February 1976 – my actual due date – that my parents could finally bring me home. Mam kept a journal of what was for her as a young mother a very difficult and emotional time, which she has since passed on to me. It is very clear from the early entries that, because I was so tiny and so early, initially I was not expected to survive. Maybe it is possible that, because I spent the first weeks of my life suspended between this world and the next, the experience in some way gave me a heightened awareness of Spirit. Whether or not this is the case, it is my belief that there is a reason why I did not cross over then – that there is a definite purpose in my being here on this earth. I believe that we are all here for a reason.

I don't remember there being anything particularly unusual about my childhood – although like everyone else's, I suppose my story is unique in its own way. My father was in the army and we lived in army quarters for the first years of my childhood. Mam was a seamstress and dressmaker, although she gave this work up once they started a family, so that she could take care of us full-time. We stayed in army accommodation in Rathmines until I was four years old, when we moved to Tallaght.

During his time in the army, my dad was often away – he did a tour in Yugoslavia and went to Lebanon a few times, and so on. He would be away for six months at a time. My mother still has the cassette tapes we sent to Dad while he was in Lebanon. We kids would record our messages for him on the 'A' side of these tapes, and once he got them and had listened to them, he would record his reply on the 'B' side and send the tapes back to us. We also kept in touch via aerograms: I remember how we would write a letter to Dad once a week on these ingenious sheets of paper and then stick down the flaps, so that the letter became its own envelope. Phone calls were few and far between, and there would be great excitement at the thought of talking to Dad 'live' on his walkie-talkie and having to remember to sign off each sentence with a very official sounding 'Over'!

My parents say they don't remember me being different to my siblings (there are four of us) in any way that indicated early on that I had mediumistic abilities –

except for the fact that, from the age of about two or three years, I would often freak them out a little by being able to recite the names of streets in Dublin city I had never been to before. To this day, I don't have an explanation for this – perhaps residual memories from some past life? Apparently around that time, too, I had a favourite expression I kept repeating – 'De fida may' – 'the fifth of May' possibly? Again, no one in the family has ever been able to work out the meaning of this self-coined phrase, or why I kept saying it, over and over.

As a child, I had imaginary friends, as a lot of children do – but I don't have any clear recollection of ever seeing any Spirit people or of being conscious that there was such a dimension to life. It's possible, however, that I did see and connect with those from the Spirit World and that the reason I have no special memory of such things is that it just seemed very normal and natural to me – which is how I experience connection with that world today. As far as imaginary friends are concerned, by the way, I am certain that these are in fact manifestations of Spirit that only children can see, because of their openness and lack of fixed ideas about how the world should be.

The first experience I clearly recall of a death in our immediate family was the passing of my dad's brother,

Declan, in 1985. I was exactly ten years old at the time, and the reason I always remember this is because Declan died on my birthday. I remember feeling great sadness at the death of my young uncle, who was only twenty-four and whose kids we spent a lot of time with growing up, since he too was in the army and was often on tour like Dad. Since I was so young, however, there was no sense as far as I can recall in which Declan's death made me reflect on the world of Spirit or heightened my awareness of such a thing.

Three years later, however, the passing of 'Granny', my great-grandmother, affected me very deeply in terms of my connection with Spirit. It was she who first appeared to me years later during the time of Richard's illness. I was very close to Granny from a young age. She was a very gentle, loving and deeply spiritual lady, who, even though she suffered from a lot of ill-health throughout her life, always had a kind word, a hug and a huge smile for her great-grandson, and I loved just spending time with her. In fact, whenever my mother would go with us once a week to see her mother (whom we kids had christened 'Nanny'), I would always skip out of the house as soon as we arrived and make my way to Granny's, which was only a five-minute walk down the road.

I believe that it was Granny, being such a spiritual lady herself, who first tapped into my affinity with Spirit, and perhaps this is one reason why we enjoyed each other's company so much. Losing her when I was just thirteen years old, however, was such a painful experience for me that in the years that followed her death, it seems that I made the decision – albeit unconsciously – to shut down the spiritually attuned part of myself which she had helped to nurture. But the longing for Spirit, which Granny had seen and encouraged in me, never truly went away.

So it was Granny and then my Uncle Richard who guided me towards the wonderful path of spiritual discovery, and for this I will be eternally grateful to both of those dear loved ones.

3

FIRST STEPS WITH THE SPIRIT WORLD

> Die happily and look forward to taking up a new and better form. Like the sun, only when you set in the west can you rise in the east.
>
> *Jalaluddin Rumi*

People are often surprised by my reply when they ask me what I did before becoming a full-time medium – which I only did in 2009, at the age of thirty-four. Some seem taken aback that I have done anything other than mediumship in my professional life. Many are even more surprised when I explain that I had a career in accountancy. I'm not sure what life path people expect a medium to have had, but I suppose what intrigues them in my case is the apparent contrast between the rational and straitlaced world of accountancy, which deals in figures and facts, and the mysterious realm of Spirit, which relies on the intuition and faith of those who seek to connect to it. Personally, I don't see such a big gulf between the two – just as I don't think that it is only special and exceptionally gifted people who have the ability to communicate with those in the Spirit World.

At school I loved the accounting aspect of the business studies course I took for the Leaving Certificate and I quickly realised that I wanted to make a career in this area. From the beginning it wasn't so much the arithmetic side, the adding and subtracting and so on, that I enjoyed – it was the problem-solving element: balancing the books, reconciling the debits and credits, making sense of how a business is working by interpreting the figures.

When I left school in 1994 I took my accounting technician diploma and by 1995 I was working full-time in ESBI (the international division of the Irish Electricity Supply Board) as an accounts assistant in their contracting division. We were tasked with looking after the monthly returns of various overseas projects, including the building of power stations in such far-flung places as Lebanon, Syria, Malaysia and South Africa. It was exciting to be involved in such foreign operations, even from a distance, and to be working with a number of different currencies.

After a few years I decided that I wanted to become a qualified chartered accountant, and since a suitable employer sponsorship arrangement wasn't on offer at ESBI, I left the company in 1996 to join the Dublin accountancy practice of Niall Brophy (the former Irish rugby international and one-time IRFU president). I greatly enjoyed my work with Niall and eventually, in 2002, we went into partnership together. At one stage, I was working a lot in the area of foreign property development, which meant frequent overseas travel, often for several weeks at a time, to locations such as the Caribbean and the USA. I loved spending time in these countries, helping to research and put together property-development projects and seeing other cultures at work. Again, it was not so much the nuts and bolts work of the accountancy side that I enjoyed – I remember dreading the approach of tax time every October! It was the challenge of making the figures work, putting together viable contracts and playing my part in helping a client's project become a reality.

However, after Richard's death in 2001 I found myself increasingly asking questions about life and in particular about what happens after we die. I had a very powerful desire to somehow make contact with the uncle I had been so close to and I had a strong intuition that somehow he was still around. I realised that I needed to find out more about the world of Spirit.

While Richard's death was a definite turning point, I can't pinpoint a precise or dramatic 'Road-to-Damascus' moment when I decided to change the whole direction of my life. I suppose I experienced more of a gradual realisation, an opening up of my spiritual awareness. In the months after Richard's passing, I began to attend the Irish Spiritual Centre in Dublin where I met Liz Homen, a spiritual healer and medium, and I started going along to her weekly spiritual development classes. This was my first formal encounter with the world of mediumship and Spirit, and I was completely enthralled by it all.

I would sit in Liz's class every Wednesday night and watch, fascinated, as with her help others in our circle connected with the Spirit World. Another thing we focused on in the group was communicating with earthbound spirits – those who for some reason have not been able to make the transition to the Spirit World and remain in this dimension. Our goal was to 'rescue' these spirits, helping them to finally cross over and find peace and contentment. I was greatly intrigued by all of this and the realisation that we could – in the words of Cole, the young boy in the film *The Sixth Sense* – 'see dead people' and connect with them in a meaningful way.

I continued with Liz's classes for about eighteen months. For the next few years after that, I kept up my involvement in the world of mediumship in a low-key way, attending various other classes and workshops here and there. I also pursued a growing interest in spiritual healing and Reiki, and did some introductory training in both. I realised that there is a strong link between mediumship and healing, which is why I wanted to learn more about various healing techniques. All this time, I was still working in my day job in the accountancy practice with Niall and thoroughly enjoying the overseas property-development work.

Then, in September 2006, a decisive encounter set me on my spiritual path once more with renewed purpose. My wife Linda and I had gone along to a public demonstration of mediumship being given by Mary Edwards, who has been working as a professional medium and spiritual counsellor since 1996. I knew that one of Mary's key areas of focus was helping people make contact with their 'Spirit guides' – these are the Spirit loved ones or other Spirit entities who, even before we come to this earth, have been chosen by us and our higher power to help and give us guidance in life. So in a way, I don't know why I was particularly surprised when at a certain point in the evening, Mary approached me to say that she had made contact with Richard and that he was present in the room. She described him to a tee and said that he was always there for me. Although I had felt for a long time that Uncle Richard was very much still around and watching over me, to get this kind of verification from someone external was a very emotional experience.

I know now that Richard is one of my Spirit guides, and to this day he remains in constant contact with me. I always know when he is trying to communicate with me, as he has his own very particular ways of making his presence felt. The number twenty-one, for example, is one of the key signs I associate with my uncle – he was born on the twenty-first of the month, he died on the twenty-first of the month, and the last car he drove was registered on the twenty-first. It is a number that comes up constantly in my life, and when it does, I know Richard is close by.

After this experience at Mary's demonstration, I decided to attend her spiritual development classes, and did so for about twelve months, during which time I was continuing to learn more about how to connect with Spirit and how to develop my own mediumship abilities.

The next important step forward for me was to set up my own development circle – but this came about as a result of happenstance rather than a conscious decision on my part. (Although of course my view is that nothing in this life happens by mere coincidence.)

Richard's death had deeply affected Mam too and in the intervening years she had studied with Dr Doreen Virtue and had obtained a qualification as an angel-therapy practitioner. After this she had attended specialist advanced training in California and in 2004 had qualified as an advanced angel-therapy practitioner. Mam's spiritual development was progressing in leaps and bounds, and the transformation in her was plain for all to see. Where she had previously been plagued by doubts and negative thoughts, she was now open and full of joy about life, and deeply connected to the world of Spirit. Mam had been able to take on board the very painful experience of nursing her brother through terminal cancer and, rather than letting it flood her with sadness and hopelessness, she had allowed it to set her on a spiritual path where she could focus on healing both others and herself.

Before, Mam had been someone who hated speaking in public and had little confidence in such situations.

By 2007 she was facilitating three different and very successful weekly angel classes in local schools, as well as doing the same type of work with a regular group in Mountjoy women's prison.

Anyway, to get back to how my development circle came about, in 2007 Mam was planning to be away on holiday for a while and asked me if I could take one of her angel classes in her absence. I said I'd be happy to oblige. Having no experience of angel therapy, however, when I took the class, I did some channelling work with them instead. Fortunately the session was a great success and the following week the number attending had increased dramatically, as word had obviously got out.

When Mam came back from holiday, she was delighted that everything had gone so well and was happy for me to continue doing a session with this group on the last Wednesday of each month. As time went on, and the numbers for that class went from strength to strength, Mam and I began to joke about having to hire out the RDS in Dublin for the class. And someday we will!

I was continuing my training in various alternative forms of healing and I successfully completed Reiki II and my Reiki Master's training, as well as the National Federation of Spiritual Healers (NFSH) Course, Parts I to IV. Meanwhile, career-wise, I had decided that after ten years working in an accountancy practice, I wanted a change and I managed to secure a position as financial controller in a large construction company in Dublin.

By now I was really enjoying my growing involvement in mediumship and spirituality, and was keen to develop my abilities further still. Here I found myself up against a bit of a brick wall, however, as I realised that in Ireland, at the time, it was very difficult to find any kind of training in advanced mediumship development. I spent many hours on the Internet, searching for courses – but all in vain. Fortunately around this time, Paddy Woods, a good friend of mine, mentioned that, at a reading he had recently been to, he had heard about a college in the UK – the Arthur Findlay College in Stansted – that specialised in mediumship studies. Delighted at this, I went online to look at the college website. As soon as I saw that there was an Advanced Mediumship Workshop coming up – in June 2008 – I signed up for a place.

The month of June that year couldn't come quickly enough. When the big day arrived, I got a Ryanair flight to Stansted Airport and took a taxi to the college, which was just a ten-minute journey from the airport. As we drove up the long, tree-lined driveway to the large, imposing main building of Stansted Hall, I could feel my excitement growing. I had arrived early, and as check-in was not until 3 p.m., I took a short walk in the picturesque countryside and got a bit of lunch in Mountfitchet, the local village. Then I returned to the college to check in.

At 4.30 p.m. all of the students for the course gathered in the main lecture hall. We were introduced to the mediumship tutors who would be coaching us for the week – Val Williams, Morag Bence and Janet Gay. I found myself particularly drawn to Morag, a small Scottish lady who reminded me of the main character in the TV programme *Super Gran*. As I took in our surroundings, I felt for all the world like Harry Potter in Hogwarts: the building had that air and feeling about it. Painted portraits of the Findlay family hung on the wall of the impressive lecture hall: I half-expected the gazing eyes looking out from the paintings to follow me around the room, like in one of those old-fashioned horror movies!

Having been given an outline of the course, what it would entail and the detailed programme for the week, we broke for dinner. Later that evening we reconvened in circle and were each given two minutes to introduce ourselves and talk about what stage we felt we were at in our mediumship development. It was really good to hear more about everybody and what each person in the group wanted to get out of the week.

The following day, in addition to attending an introductory lecture and some platform work (where a medium goes on stage and connects to Spirit in a group setting) by Val, the course organiser, I had booked a one-to-one session with Morag Bence. I was keen for her to give me an assessment of what stage I was at in my spiritual development. Morag was able to tell me quite quickly that, as far as my ability to connect with Spirit went, I had developed a block in my early teens, around the time of the death of a close relative. Before this, it seemed, I had been able to communicate with the Spirit World. I now asked Spirit to help me get to the next level and break down the fear – and, at this point, Granny came through via Morag! Granny confirmed that she was one of my main Spirit guides and would be helping me to overcome the barriers within me that were blocking the flow of my mediumship.

The next day we got stuck into the course in earnest, beginning with a session with Morag. She talked us through the difference between meditation and attunement – namely that meditation deals with calming the physical aspect, whereas attunement relates to initiating the connection with the Spirit World. Each of us then set about doing our own attunement exercises, after which we were given feedback by Morag. She confirmed that I was indeed beginning to attune, but said that I was only just scratching the surface and that I still had a long way to go before being able to overcome the resistance to the communication process being created by my conscious mind.

That afternoon we did a very interesting exercise aimed at heightening our senses. The exercise involved working in pairs, with one of us closing our eyes and allowing our partner to lead us around the gardens of the college. The idea was that we would experience our surroundings through sound and touch only. We were to remain silent throughout. This was a very educational exercise because you had to put your complete trust in the person who was guiding you around and rely totally on your other senses to 'see'.

I found that not being able to see as usual did indeed mean that my other senses took over. I felt the air on my hands, and in my mind's eye (also known as the 'third eye') I could see vibrant colours, as well as the symbol of a large eye, exactly like the *Big Brother* logo. At one point, my partner in the exercise, Ben, brought me over to a tree and placed my hands on its trunk, asking me to use my connection with Spirit to say how old it was. Instantaneously the words 'three years old' came into my mind. Ben, who in fact worked with trees in his day job, confirmed that my dating of the tree was about right.

As the week progressed we had a session focusing on inspirational speaking. This entailed choosing a subject and talking about it off-the-cuff. Ideally, our inspiration was to come from those in the Spirit World, so that the information would just flow. To guide us in our choice of topic, we each had to draw angel cards. I found that I had chosen a card of peace. Although I had been quite apprehensive when contemplating this task, once I stood up I found that I was able to talk quite fluently. I spoke about the North/South divide in Ireland: about how for many years people had not been getting on because they saw each other as different; about how it only took one person who decided change was needed and set the wheels in motion to start a change in the process. I could not believe how easily and eloquently I was speaking – but of course I was channelling the wisdom of Spirit, and so my words were not my own.

It was an emotional speech and afterwards some of the others told me that as I had been speaking, they could see that my energy was increasing, as well as the volume of my voice, while I also appeared to get bigger in physical appearance. People mentioned, too, that at one point during my time on the stage there had been quite a long pause: it was as if Spirit was making us all aware of the sound of silence: the sound of peace.

As the week progressed, my confidence in my own abilities and instincts was growing all the time. It was as if all that I had learned over the years was somehow coming together in a culmination of understanding and acceptance. On the last day of the course we each had to do a platform demonstration in front of the whole group – a nerve-racking prospect for everyone. The majority of us had very little experience of platform work and, in spite of the atmosphere of mutual support and encouragement within our group, we all knew that this would be a real test of everything we had learned during the week – and of whether we had any promise as mediums or otherwise.

By the time it was my turn to get up on platform, I was extremely nervous. But I knew that what I needed to do above all was to try to keep myself in a relaxed and receptive state, otherwise my efforts to connect would not be successful. So I calmed myself and started to attune to the Spirit World, drawing on some of the techniques we had learned that very week. Soon I felt a gentleman, a young girl and an older lady draw close to me. 'I have three Spirit communicators here,' I said. 'I will start with the older lady.' I began to give the information that was coming through to me about this lady and asked if anyone understood the connection. But I was met with silence and a sea of blank, uncomprehending faces. It seemed that no one was able to acknowledge what I had said.

I wasn't about to give up, however. I asked the lady to stand back and then focused my attention on the gentleman, beckoning him to come forward. Again, I began to pass on to the group all the details that were coming into my mind, asking if anyone could make a connection. Yet again, there was only silence from those in front of me: no one was able to take the information.

By now, I was beginning to feel really unnerved – but something told me to persist. The connection felt very real to me, and I had no choice but to go with my intuition and follow through. I asked the gentleman to stand back and now asked the young girl to come forward. Once more, information began to come through, clear and precise. But when I gave the details to my audience, again there were no takers: no one could relate to any of what I was saying. By this time I had been about fifteen minutes up on the platform, although, to me, it felt like I had been standing up there forever with these three Spirit people whom no one understood.

I was beginning to wonder what on earth I should do next, when Val, one of the course tutors, put her hand up. 'Tom, I understand all of the information. I just wanted to see where you went with it before letting you know I could take it.' *Thank God for that*, I thought. And now that I had this validation from Val, I was quickly able to refocus on the three Spirit presences beside me.

The young girl stepped forward and said to me, 'Look at all of these individual pieces of material, all different colours and different sizes like a jigsaw, but if you put them all together and look at the beauty they create, you can see the bigger picture.' I relayed this information to Val. She smiled and nodded. 'At the end of every workshop,' she said, 'I ask each of the students to take a piece of coloured material from a treasure chest, and then we put them all together to see what we can create – in this way, we look at the bigger picture. So that is a very good piece of evidence of Spirit connection, Tom. Thank you!' I was delighted with myself. I had persisted because I knew the Spirit communicators that I had beside me were strong energies and I was convinced that the information they were giving me was correct. I think I was up on the platform for about twenty minutes in total, but it had felt far, far longer!

After the demonstration session, a few of my fellow students came up to me and congratulated me for my perseverance. 'I'm sure I would have been mortified,' one of them said. 'I'd have just sat down again straight away when no one took the information!'

This final experience of what had been a truly inspiring week gave me a huge sense of confidence, which I was able to carry into many future situations. On occasions when I feel I am making a strong, true connection to Spirit but find that none of the information I am giving is being picked up by anyone in the room, I am able to think back to that first time on platform and remember the importance of persistence and having faith in my abilities and in Spirit.

By the autumn of 2008 I was keen to put my newly acquired knowledge and confidence to the test in front of the most critical audience of all – the general public. I made plans to do my first solo public demonstration on 12 October in the Ballyfermot Civic Centre in Dublin. By that stage, of course, I already had a bit of previous experience leading circle groups and classes, as well as with private readings (although I had only felt ready to start doing such readings outside of a circle or class context in 2007, after six years of involvement in the field). But other than the platform performance at the Arthur Findlay College, I had never appeared on stage as a demonstrating medium before the public. It was a daunting prospect.

At the course we had each had the support and encouragement of like-minded fellow students and our dedicated tutors, whereas the general public, I knew, wouldn't take any prisoners or be overly sympathetic if they felt I wasn't coming up with results quickly enough – particularly at an event they had paid money to attend, an event I organised. I feel I should make it clear that, while not unimportant for my livelihood, the financial reward has never been the main element of my motivation in doing public mediumship events. What drives me above all is a desire to share my insights with others and to bring to them the knowledge and healing for which I can be a channel, by making contact with loved ones who have passed over. Undertaking this type of work has also been an important way for me to continue to develop my mediumship abilities and grow in experience, confidence and understanding.

Luckily, I got a lot of support from colleagues, friends and family in preparing for the Ballyfermot event. Rob Wright and Dolores Malone (now Mr and Mrs Wright), both members of my development circle, were a great help in selling tickets, as was my mother, Ann, at her classes. I knew there had been a lot of interest from the public in the run-up to the event, but even so, I was delighted and very pleasantly surprised when a crowd of 120 people turned up to see me on the big day. I realised that I would need to draw on every ounce of confidence I had gained at the course to be able to carry off the next few hours with any degree of success.

As I stood in the wings just before going out on stage, I was a bundle of nerves. But I forced myself to focus, calling upon all my Spirit guides and loved ones to be with me and to stay with me throughout this demonstration, which was so important to me. And they definitely didn't let me down. As I did reading after reading, I was able to sharpen my concentration and relax into the state of attunement I needed to connect fully and effectively with Spirit. With each minute that passed my information got clearer and more precise, and was being picked up consistently by audience members. And I could feel a shift in the mood of the crowd, as a series of people responded to confirm the details I was bringing through. An initial sense of doubt and wariness in the audience was now giving way to a feeling of acceptance and growing excitement.

At this first demonstration, not all of the details and information I brought forward could be immediately verified or acknowledged as relevant by the individuals in question. But, thanks to my training at the college and the personal insights I had gained over the years through my work, I knew that this was not unusual and I didn't need to panic or to assume that what had come through was inaccurate or irrelevant. On this occasion, as in so many which were to come, it was only in the days that followed that various people got in touch to let me know that what I had said made sense after all.

One such case had to do with a reading where a mother came through very clearly to her daughter in the audience – this Spirit lady was singing the song 'Paper Roses' as she came into my awareness. I was able to pass on information she gave me about her husband and a set of golf clubs he had recently bought, just to be able to say he had a set in the house. He had never actually played golf: he just thought it looked good to be seen to own a set of clubs! All of this her daughter was able to verify immediately. Then, however, the mother came through again, this time with an image of Moore Street in Dublin where the market traders sell fruit, vegetables, flowers and fish, after which she showed me the shop front of Tyrell's butchers (which I knew myself, as the Tyrell family had at one point been accounting clients of mine). 'Your mam is making reference to a member of the family actually working on Moore Street,' I said.

'Oh really? I don't think so,' the daughter replied. 'We used to go to Moore Street to buy fruit and vegetables, but I'm pretty sure none of us has ever worked there.'

Nothing daunted, I asked her to see if she could verify the information after the demonstration and if possible, to let me know if she had any update. Sure enough, a couple of days later, the same lady rang me to say that she had checked with her grandmother and yes, in fact, it was true after all – her great-grandfather had owned a butcher's shop on Moore Street! It wasn't Tyrell's butchers, though – but her Spirit loved one had worked with the references that were familiar to me to evoke the idea of a butcher's shop.

The accuracy of the information I am able to bring through for people is in fact the cornerstone of the type of mediumship I practise – 'evidential mediumship'. I will be looking at this issue of information and its accuracy later, and why it is so important. But suffice to say for now that such detail is the means by which a Spirit loved one who wants to make contact with someone will prove to that person that they are who they claim to be, and that the communication is genuine and something to be trusted.

Buoyed up by the success of the Ballyfermot event, I decided to go back to the Arthur Findlay College in December 2008 to do a Spiritualists' National Union (SNU) Platform Accreditation weekend. I was keen to formalise my presentation and mediumship skills in this context and when I arrived I discovered that my tutor for the weekend was to be Morag Bence! I was thrilled. The inspiration and encouragement Morag offered, and the knowledge that she so generously shared with all of us on that first week's course at the college, and indeed at various training events ever since, is something I will never forget.

On 16 February 2009, I hosted my second demonstration at the Civic Centre in Ballyfermot and, once again, had a very good turnout. This event was equally, if not more, successful than the first, although in some ways very different for me. By this, I mean that my connections were stronger, and information flowed more quickly and was more focused, which helped to establish an even more intense connection with Spirit.

In fact I didn't fully realise this myself until afterwards, when a number of people commented on the fact that, while I was channelling, my face had changed at various points throughout the night, taking on the expression and appearance of the different people I was in contact with. At the time, I wasn't aware of this – all I knew was that I was able to make a really strong connection with some of the Spirit people who presented themselves to me.

As a medium, you never stop learning about the Spirit World and the different ways and techniques through which it can be accessed. If any medium tells you they know everything and have learned all there is to learn, then, in my opinion, they are not embracing the Spirit World in its truest form. I have always been keen to keep building on my knowledge and experience of the world of Spirit. In April 2009 I returned to the Arthur Findlay College again, along with six members of my circle, to attend 'Standing Up for Spirit' – a week-long course being delivered by Tony Stockwell. Tony is an established authority in the world of mediumship and has a high public profile in the UK and beyond. He has worked extensively in the media and has had numerous television series, including *Psychic Detective*, *Street Psychic* and *Psychic Academy*. He also appeared as a regular guest on Colin Fry's *6ixth Sense*.

As far as that week at Tony's course goes, all I can say is *Wow*! What a great, down-to-earth guy he is, so dedicated to Spirit and with such a beautiful nature and manner. His way of helping others understand the Spirit World in easy, everyday language, with an air of humour to it all, gave me an insight into another method of working with Spirit – one which I could relate to very well, being someone who prefers to stay as grounded as possible and enjoys a laugh now and then too.

Thanks to my very positive experiences with platform work, and the courses I had done, my confidence was growing all the time. I held a third public demonstration on 2 June 2009 in the Civic Theatre in Tallaght. It was on this occasion that for the first time I introduced an element for my audience which I would later refer to as 'feel the energy of your loved one the way a medium does'. The basic idea was to work with individual audience members and transfer directly to them the energy that was being channelled to me by their Spirit loved ones. The results were very dramatic and striking, with subjects (or 'sitters') assuming the expressions or physical mannerisms of their Spirit loved ones and afterwards reporting having profound feelings of love and positive energy during the process.

By the summer of 2009 my mediumship demonstrations, training and other related activities were taking up more and more of my time and energy. I experienced this only as a positive thing: I was loving the work and felt strongly that it was what I had been put on this earth to do. I knew I had made huge progress in terms of my abilities and confidence, as I always felt a tremendous surge of energy and sense of purpose each time I gave a successful public demonstration – a feeling that would last for days afterwards.

There had also been another very exciting development. A group of us who had studied together at the Arthur Findlay College decided to set up the Spiritualist Union of Ireland (SUI) and in June 2009 the Sanctuary (the church of the Spiritualist Union of Ireland where we hold our weekly service and development classes) had opened its doors to the public, the first church of its kind in the Republic of Ireland. (I will talk more about the founding of the SUI in Chapter 12.) I was continuing to do my day job of course, but I knew my real energy and focus were now elsewhere, and I was beginning to wonder if I needed to seriously consider reassessing the career path I had taken to date.

As it turned out, a series of events soon sparked a major change in my life – as we all know, by mid-2009 Ireland was deep in recession. The sector in which I was working was one of the worst affected areas of the economy of all. On 8 June 2009 – just days after my third public demonstration in Tallaght – I was told that my accountancy job was being cut from five days a week to three. I wasn't despondent at this news, however. In fact, the feeling I had was something very different: I was delighted! Here was my chance to work more on my mediumship.

Of course I was concerned about the financial side of things, but my overriding feeling was one of excitement. Over the days that followed, I spent a lot of time reflecting and tuning in to the Spirit World. I soon found myself saying to Spirit: 'If you want me to work full-time in mediumship, helping people realise that they can communicate with you, then give me some kind of sign. Show me that's what I should be doing!' Two days later, I got a phone call out of the blue from a guy saying he had heard a lot about what I was doing and that he was looking for a medium to take part in events around the country at a number of venues that he had already booked. Although

I wasn't to be the sole presenter in the demonstrations he had in mind, he went on to explain that, if I took up the opportunity, he would need a full-time commitment from me over a number of months. I was blown away by this. If this wasn't a verification of Spirit at work, I didn't know what was!

In the end I didn't actually take up this opportunity, as a few days later, when we met, and in further discussions we had after that, it soon became clear that we had very different ideas about mediumship and how to relate to the public. But the fact that he had got in touch when he did had served its purpose and gave me the push I needed to decide to focus on being a full-time, professional medium. Another knock-on effect was that I soon afterwards did a series of mediumship events myself and put together the 'Feel the Spirit' tour – the first of its kind ever to be undertaken by an Irish medium. The seventeen-date tour took in all four corners of the country, and ran over five months, beginning in Cavan in July and climaxing with several special 'Christmas With Spirit' dates in Dublin, Waterford and Cork. It was a whirlwind adventure in many ways, after which my full-time career in the world of mediumship was well and truly launched.

~

To this day, I am convinced that my Uncle Richard's passing was meant to happen at the time it did, according to his sacred contract, and that his death in turn became one of a sequence of events which helped to set me on the spiritual path I needed to be on. I was thereby able to discover my true purpose in life: channelling of Spirit and, through this, bringing healing to as many people as possible and sharing with them the truth from Spirit that there is something for us all beyond physical death. I use the term 'physical death', as I know that our spirit is an eternal life form, and that dying in the physical form is really just like starting a new chapter in the book of our existences.

4

I HAVEN'T GONE ANYWHERE – I HAVE JUST MOVED ON

> After death we are not disembodied spirits. Somewhere in God's wonderful creation there is a place, where we can again be with those we have loved and lost for a while.
>
> *C. L. Allen*

People think that because you are a medium, it somehow doesn't affect you when someone close to you passes. It does. You still go through the emotional roller coaster and the grieving, the physical loss of the loved one. While in some respects it makes it easier when you know there is another place we go to when our physical body passes, the pain and sorrow at the time of the loss are just as intense.

In March 2012 we lost my aunt, my mother's sister

Mary, to the Spirit World. Mary Kealy was born in Arbour Hill Army quarters, the ninth child of my maternal grandparents, Butch and Peg (Henry and Margaret are their actual names, but they are known in the family as Butch and Peg). As can be imagined, things were already hectic within the family unit, but straight away Mary won the affection of her father and quickly became daddy's girl – a fact that Butch would always deny, but she could do no wrong in his eyes. Everyone knew she was his favourite, and she would remain so until the day she passed away.

At school and elsewhere, Mary always seemed to be a magnet for like-minded people – by which I mean people who were determined to live life to the full – and she was a vibrant, outgoing and fun-loving person. Mary was not only a daddy's girl, she also had a very close relationship with her mother, whom she referred to as 'the social worker', as she always confided in her and asked her advice. And in fact, Mary had two mammies, the other one being her mother-in-law, Laurie. Mary loved everything about Laurie – her personality, her faith, her cooking. Mary's love for her husband Seán, her children, Shaunagh and Jack, and her family and friends was, and is, passionate and immense.

The first sign that anything was wrong was when Mary started to experience intense headaches, which the doctors quickly diagnosed as migraines. The headaches got worse, however, and she had various tests done. My uncle, Tony, and my sister, Anita, were there in Beaumont Hospital with Mary when the doctor delivered the details of Mary's prognosis. It was the news none of us wanted to hear. She had a glioblastoma – a cancerous tumour in the brain – and she had, at best, eighteen months to live. As it turned out, it was just four months: four months of hell.

During the time of Mary's illness, her father Butch, my grandfather, was in hospital with a condition called Lewy body, which is a form of dementia. He is still in full-time care to this day. Just a couple of days before Mary passed, another aunt was up visiting Butch, and at one point he turned around to her and said, 'I have given Mary the pass to cross the border – I don't need it anymore: they know me from going back and forward.' In the case of people with dementia, it is my belief that their Spirit body often leaves the physical body for periods of time, to wander elsewhere – which gives the impression that their mind is not all it should be. If they seem to be somehow absent at times, perhaps it is because, literally, they are – these are the times when their Spirit body is absent from their physical body.

The same aunt who had visited Butch that day remembers being with Mary in hospital on one occasion, when all at once Mary began to wave out at the corridor. My aunt asked her who she was waving at. 'I'm waving at my da,' Mary replied.

'Where is he?' my aunt said. 'I don't see him anywhere.'

'He's out there – are you blind?' said Mary. All of this ties in with my belief that Butch's spirit is often wandering far from his physical body: on this occasion Mary could see my grandfather's spirit, even though he was physically in a different hospital.

I remember very clearly the day Mary passed. It was 21 March 2012. I was out on the playing fields in North Kildare Hockey Club, umpiring a hockey game. I had already had a call to say that the close family had been called to the hospital. It was coming up to the end of the first half and I looked at my watch – twenty-one seconds left. As I have said, the number twenty-one is my sign from Richard, so I knew at that moment that Mary had passed. A couple of moments later, my phone rang: it was Mam's number. As soon as the game finished, I rang her back and she told me that Mary was no longer with us.

The number of people that turned up to my aunt's funeral proved just how much she was loved. All of them wanted to be there to bid farewell to this vivacious, vibrant lady, and each one had their own stories to tell about her, many of which were shared over the days which followed. Mary touched so many people in her own special way. Her heart was huge and she always looked for the good in everyone.

On the day of the funeral the church was packed to capacity, and well beyond, with people standing out in the car park. I was asked to read a piece about Mary that her brother Tony had written. In my role as Minister of the Spiritualist Union of Ireland, I have officiated at funerals, as well as many weddings and naming ceremonies, so speaking to large crowds of people isn't usually a problem for me. However, when it is one of your own, it is so different. This speech was one of the hardest I have ever had to give. I asked Mary and my other loved ones in Spirit to give me the strength to get through Tony's reflection on her life and to do her justice in the way I delivered it. I asked them to help me hold back the emotion for long enough so that I could read out my uncle's words.

Mary's loss was a body blow to our whole family, just as the loss of anyone dear is to those who loved them. In my extended family we have experienced the death of family members all too often. Mary, my aunt, was the fourth child of Peg and Butch to have gone back to the Spirit World ahead of them. Their daughter Lisa was stillborn; Richard, my uncle and Spirit guide, died in 2001, at the age of thirty-nine; Harry died of liver failure in the same year at the age of forty-one; and in 2012 it was Mary.

So as I have said, being a working medium certainly doesn't dull the pain of loss in some ways, as some people might expect. But the knowledge that one day I will be reunited with all of the loved ones who have gone before me is a huge consolation, and being able to connect with the Spirit World and my Spirit loved ones in the here and now gives me great comfort. My spiritual beliefs, which are constantly being affirmed by all of my experiences as a medium, enable me to look beyond the immediate sense of loss and see things in a bigger context.

When a loved one passes over, especially when it seems to us that they have died before their time, the first question that we ask ourselves is: 'Why? Why were they taken from me? Why *me*?' But we need to remember that it is also about the person who has passed over. If they had completed their sacred contract, then it was their time to pass over. Nothing we do or say can change this. When it's your time to go back to the Spirit World, it's your time. This can be very hard for us to accept when we have lost someone close. But everything is in divine and perfect order. My belief is that what is meant to happen will happen, and that, as human beings, we have limited or no control over these things.

~

Sometimes, it is only with the passage of time that the reasons for the challenges we are faced with become clear. We have rainy days. When we get a rainy day, the clouds hide the sun. But we need the rain, so all of the plants and trees can grow. And even when rain clouds cover the sun and we can't see it, we know that it is there. The same can be said of the Spirit World. Just as the sun energises and touches us, so do those in the Spirit World with their encouragement, help and wisdom. We need to look past the dark clouds and see the sunshine that never goes away.

Some time ago, a lady called Sarah came along to my monthly development circle. It was her first time there and my first time meeting her. A friend of hers had told her about the work I was doing, having seen an ad I had placed in a magazine called *Natural Connections*.

I started the session by doing some Spirit work with the group, and then moved on to some readings. Sarah didn't ask for a reading, but I was drawn to ask her to come and sit on the chair at the front of the room, which I always have in place for sitters. Willingly, she did so. Very soon, as I started to connect, Sarah's son Brendan came through. He was now in the Spirit World, and I got a strong sense that he had passed as a young child.

Brendan told me that he shared a name with another member of his family who was also in the Spirit World. This didn't make sense to Sarah at the time – but later she was able to tell me that Brendan shared his second name with an uncle. Now I could also see an eighteen- to twenty-year-old guy, but there were several things I couldn't understand at the time. First, I couldn't sense any pain, something I normally would feel from a spirit's passing over. So this was unusual. It didn't make sense in relation to either Brendan or the older presence I could sense. I asked the young Spirit man if he had died through crossing himself over, but he said no. And at the time, since I didn't know about Brendan's connection with the uncle through a shared name, the other thing I couldn't understand was why I was getting such a strong sense of the presence of an older guy when, as Sarah had now told me, Brendan had passed in his sleep at the age of six months.

Next, baby Brendan gave me a few signals to pass on to

Sarah, in order to confirm his identity. He told me that he kept turning off a CD that his mam had in the kitchen: Sarah was able to confirm that the CD in question was a Tina Turner album she was listening to a lot at the time. Now Brendan was telling his mother to listen instead to the CD of dolphin sounds that she had purchased the previous week, to raise her 'vibration' (attunement to Spirit). Next Brendan wanted me to mention the family dog – a small dog, which Sarah confirmed was a terrier – and his habit of barking into one of the corners in the kitchen. This, too, Sarah was able to confirm. Brendan told her that it was *him* 'the little mutt' (to use Brendan's words) was barking at all the time.

This was the first time that a medium working with Sarah had picked up Brendan and his energy, and she was elated to have at last connected with him. The older presence I could sense around Brendan was an uncle who had acted like a father figure to him – this spirit communicated to me that the number twelve was associated with him, and Sarah was later able to confirm that the uncle who had died so young had driven the number 12 bus in Dublin. The reason that I had felt no pain around the death of baby Brendan was that he had died without a struggle, in his sleep – Sarah confirmed that it had been cot death.

The love that Brendan emitted was unbelievable – the feeling in my heart was huge. It seemed that the room kept getting warmer and warmer, and other class members said that they, too, could feel the intensity of the child's love in the air around us. Brendan told me that he had chosen to enter his mam's life to get her back on to her spiritual path. His message was that we choose our family and loved ones before we come here. He explained that, in life, he had been an incarnate guide to Sarah, and that he was now her Spirit guide from the other side, always there for her. He needed me to let his mother know that this was the case: his exact words were these: 'I haven't gone anywhere – I have just moved on.'

Hearing all of this, Sarah was very moved – as were all of us who were there. She explained that she had never been able to understand why Brendan had passed over. She told us that she had also lost a daughter to spina bifida at the age of six months and had had a miscarriage before that. (The spirit of the miscarried child was present with Brendan during the session.)

Now, however, Sarah is able to accept and better comprehend why Brendan passed over. What he told her about his purpose in life made sense, for she had indeed found a new spiritual direction after he left this life.

She got involved in healing and angel work, and is now helping many people. She does, for example, relaxation and meditation classes once a week with teenagers who are doing their final state exams before going to college. Since she started the classes, she has been receiving a lot of encouraging feedback from teachers at the school, who have told her of the really positive changes they have been able to see in the teenagers she works with.

The day after we channelled Brendan, Sarah also told me that, two and a half years previously, she had been diagnosed with breast cancer. She related how, when she was told that she had cancer, she had put together a list of important things she wanted to do for herself and others. One of these was to have a holiday home in Wexford, where she could retreat and spend time. Only because of the illness did she set about trying to achieve these goals, many of which she has now made happen. In the meantime, she was also able to make a full recovery from the cancer. As I have said above, often we truly don't know the reasons for our challenges, but in time, these can become clearer. In Sarah's case, it seems that the almost unbearable challenges of losing three precious children and being told she had cancer were what propelled her forward onto her predetermined path. While it can be terribly difficult to deal with the grief, the anger, the roller-coaster ride of emotions and the interminable questions that follow the death of a loved one, the truth is that it is only when we are in deep crisis that we turn to our faith or spirituality for answers.

~

Some people are puzzled at the idea that anyone would want to make contact with those who have passed beyond this earthly life. I am often asked by such people what the purpose of mediumship can possibly be. What am I, and those I work with, hoping to achieve in trying to establish a connection with the Spirit World? While this is not true of everyone who questions why people want to communicate with those in the Spirit World, often it is the case that those who ask such questions have not as yet experienced for themselves what it is like to lose someone close. Most people who have had this experience will understand how difficult it can be to accept the apparent fact that they may never see their loved one again. They will also be able to identify with the sheer longing felt by many of the bereaved to make some kind of connection again with the one who has gone.

While researching this book, I put the following

questions to a number of people: if you could talk to a loved one who has passed to the Spirit World, would you take the opportunity and how do you think it would make you feel to do so? And if you didn't want to take the opportunity, why not?

Here are some of the answers I received:

> I would talk to my gran every single day if I could. Twenty-one years have passed and it still feels like yesterday. I don't know how I would feel, but I have so much to tell her …

~

> My mum died nearly fifteen years ago, my boyfriend died two years ago. I wasn't with them when they passed and I'd just like [to get the chance] to say I love them both and miss them so much.

~

> I would love to speak to my little boy. He would be three this year. He passed away at six weeks old. I would ask if he was okay and tell him that his mummy, daddy, brother and sister love and miss him so much.

~

I would love to speak to my brother. He was shot last year. We weren't speaking at the time … I prayed he'd pull through, so he would know I love him and didn't want him to go. I'll have to live with this for the rest of my life.

~

Yes, [I would want to talk to] my son, who was sixteen when he passed. I would ask him if he knew that I love him more than life itself, and I would ask him if I could have saved him … and also for his forgiveness for not being there when he really needed me. I would also ask him how his baby brother is – if he is with him and safe.

~

Of course I would. I know that they are around me a lot of the time, but it would be amazing to hear what they have to say about what is going on in my life right now. Even after twenty plus years, it's still hard because we miss the physical side of them, if you know what I mean. I would love to hear from my mum and dad and big brother again.

~

This is a yes and no for me. Yes, I'd talk to all my family in the Spirit World, to ask questions about my family history and to spend valuable time with them. However, it would [also] be a no, because I have very loved ones in the Spirit World, and wouldn't want to go through the heartbreak of being separated from them again.

~

[It would have to be] my mam, who passed away in 1997. I was holding her hand when she passed, but I miss her so much. She was my rock when I needed her – she was there to help me when I was ill. So much is going on in my life now but I don't know what to do …

~

Yes, because no other person knows my pain and my worries. I would do anything to have a clear message from them … I feel like an orphan since they died, with no one to understand me like they did. I just would love to hear their opinions on how I [have] handled the last few years … and [for them] to warn me about what's coming next.

~

I can feel my family in Spirit around me all the time. My mum and grandmother are two of my guides, but I do miss their hugs.

~

It would have to be my daughter. I had to have fertility treatment to get pregnant after trying for eight years, but sadly I lost her due to an incompetent cervix. I've always blamed myself and can't get over the loss of her. I would love to let her know how sorry I was and how much I love and miss her every single day. I would like to know if she is happy and has met up with other family members.

~

I talk to my loved ones when I want … knowing that they are there keeps me going. I'm very interested in life after death – I read lots of books on the subject and I've learnt so much. I used to be scared about death, but now I know I will see my loved ones when it's my time to go.

~

For me it would be my baby boy who I carried for the full forty weeks after waiting twenty years for him. He was stillborn right on his given birth date. Many years ago I also lost a baby at twelve weeks. I don't have any kids but plenty of nieces and nephews. I do have his photos and hand and footprints. He was perfect. It was my high blood pressure and so on at the end that caused the damage to his umbilical cord. Sad, sad times. I hope he's okay and with all his relations. What bothered me was that I did not take a cutting of his beautiful hair – I don't know why.

~

I would take that precious opportunity with open arms – to see my dad and just hold him. It would be a very emotional moment, one that I would treasure forever.

~

I would want to talk to my brother who passed in 2005, and I would feel so fulfilled after doing so because of the way things were between us before he passed.

Mediumship and Spirit communication can help bring together once more that which, through death, seems to have been lost: the physical presence of those who have passed, and the love and relationships we had with them. In all of my experiences working as a medium, one truth shines brightly through: that communicating with Spirit loved ones can be a tremendous source of comfort, closure and, most especially, healing for the bereaved. I have often seen loved ones reaching across the doorway of life to tell those who are still here how sorry they are for the errors of the past, and I have been lucky enough to witness the amazing sense of healing this brings for all concerned – both on this earth plane and in the Spirit World.

Although I do not believe that death will suddenly give us a full understanding of life's mysteries, it does change things. Spirits see things from a different perspective to those of us who are still here, and as such they will have a great desire to tell their earthly loved ones what they have come to see and how they have changed since their passing. The fact that after death an individual will awaken in the Spirit World and continue to exist on that plane is the most incredible revelation in itself.

It is a true blessing to be able to help people connect with their loved ones and see the transformational change which can happen within the space of just a few hours – from someone whose face is sad and whose head hangs down dejectedly, to a new person, grinning like a Cheshire cat who is radiant with happiness. This is what evidential mediumship is all about: proving that our spirit continues to live on, even after our physical body has stopped functioning; helping those in mourning to make contact with the spirit of loved ones; allowing those in the Spirit World in turn to connect with the person who has been bereaved by inhabiting their body, so that they can feel the energy of the ones who have passed, and experience the intensity of their love. The only way I can describe this phenomenon is that it is like the scene in the film *Ghost*, where the medium (played by Whoopi Goldberg) allows the Spirit person (Patrick Swayze) to take over her body with his energy, so that he can communicate with his loved one (Demi Moore).

I cannot think about the healing, transformative power that connection with Spirit can bring, without remembering the story of one of my sitters, whom I will refer to here as Kenneth.[2] Although this encounter happened some time ago, the memory of that amazing feeling of love and connection, which all of us in the room felt, has not faded with time.

On the day in question, a family of three people had come to one of my development circles for a first visit. Although I had never seen the man of the family, I did recognise the two ladies with him – they had lived in the house next door to us when I was still living with my parents, some twenty years previously. It had been a good fifteen years since I had seen them, but I remembered their names and said hello to one of them, Aoife. She

2 All names have been changed in this and other stories of a sensitive nature.

didn't recognise me, however. Although we had lived as neighbours for a long time, both families had pretty much kept to themselves, apart from saying hello when passing in the street or nearby. (I was later told that Aoife's brother Kenneth, who didn't recognise me, had turned around to her when I greeted her by name and said, 'God, he is good, isn't he? He knew your name!' I found this very funny!)

The three sat down and Aoife's sister, Bridgit, showed me a picture on a memorial card: it was a photo of their mother, Jane. Earlier, before they had come to the class and when I had been setting up the room, I got a strong sense of a female presence, along with a male energy with the initial 'P' – possibly Peter or Paul, I thought. I hadn't been sure who the female energy was at the time and I hadn't tried to connect with it, as I knew I had to get ready for the class. But now, looking at Jane's picture, the initial 'P' in association with the female energy from earlier made sense to me. I still felt, however, that the male presence also had a connection to the initial 'P'.

I told Aoife, Bridgit and Kenneth the story of the energies I had picked up and asked if they could connect the initial 'P' with a male loved one in Spirit who was somehow linked to their mam. They said no. I had also, earlier and again now, picked up a pain in my chest and in the liver area – when I mentioned this to them, they said that it was something that made sense to them. Conscious that I had to get the class underway, I left them then, and continued greeting the circle members as they arrived. I noted, however, that I had felt particularly drawn to Kenneth, sensing that he had some kind of heightened mediumistic ability.

We began the session by doing my 'Meet Your Spirit Guide' meditation. This meditation helps those who are seeking to connect with Spirit to calm and focus their mind and energies, and takes them on a journey to a beautiful island where their Spirit guides wait for them. As I took the group through the meditation, I could sense all the while that Kenneth's mam was with him. Getting to my feet, I stood with my two hands pointing towards Kenneth, in order to send him energy and keep his mother's energy around him. I felt that there was a lot of unresolved emotion and anger inside him, although he gave no outward sign of it.

Once the meditation was finished, I specifically asked Kenneth if he was okay and if he had experienced anything. He said no. I knew, however, that during the reading sessions, which we were going to move on to next, I really needed to get him into the sitter's chair at the front, so that I could try to help him understand what had happened in the meditation. The reason I use the chair is so that everyone in the class can see what is happening and can see physical changes in a sitter, as the spirit of their loved one enters their energy field to connect with them.

As we moved on to the reading sessions, I asked the class who wanted to sit in the chair. I looked towards Aoife, Bridgit and Kenneth, and they started to discuss among themselves which one of them should go to the front. I quickly interrupted, saying, 'I really feel that Kenneth needs to sit in the chair.' He agreed, albeit a bit reluctantly, as did his two sisters.

From what I had seen, Kenneth seemed to be an introverted type of guy, who kept himself to himself. I certainly could not recall him from fifteen years before, or picture him as a child at the time. He had come into the class with his head bowed, and gave the impression that he was a shy, reserved person; the expression on his face was by turns sad or indifferent.

Anyway, Kenneth sat in the chair and I told him to relax. He settled himself and I began to ask him questions about the meditation. 'When you went on the meditation to meet your Spirit guide, Kenneth, did you go up to the house?'

'Yes,' he replied.

'Did someone open the door to you when you arrived?'

'Yes.'

'Did you see who was at the door?'

'Not really.'

'I think you did,' I said, 'because I saw who opened the door to you. Who was it?'

'I think it was my ma.'

'You think?'

'It was my ma.'

'You have spoken to her before and her to you, but you thought it was your mind creating thoughts, didn't you?'

He admitted that this had been the case. He was by now very connected. 'Okay,' I said. 'Do you want to connect with your mam now?'

'Yes,' he said, with his head still bowed.

'She is standing at your right shoulder. Can you sense her?'

'It is very hot and warm in here,' Kenneth said suddenly.

I acknowledged the presence of Jane, Kenneth's mother, and brought through some evidential details from her that he was able to confirm. I then invited Kenneth to ask a question. In my own mind, I could hear his question: he was asking his mam why she had left him. Her response, which I was also able to hear, was very interesting. She said to him, 'The reason I left was because I can do more to help you from where I am now – more than I could when I was alive.' She then confirmed that she was his Spirit guide. After this I talked to Jane for a while and she told me things about Kenneth, which again he was able to verify – such as the fact that he hadn't dealt with her passing, that he was full of anger and pain and needed to let this go so that he could move forward.

Then I asked Kenneth's sisters if they wanted to ask their mother questions. One of them asked Jane if she was all right. I asked Kenneth if he could give me the answer. 'I'm fine,' he was able to say. 'I'm fine. Don't worry about me.' He was hearing his mother, channelling his mother.

One of his sisters then said, 'Ask Mam how Paul is.' There it was: the acknowledgement of the initial 'P' and the verification of the male energy that had come in while I was setting up. None of the siblings had thought of the name earlier, when I had been asking them. Paul was their uncle – Jane's brother – who had also passed to the

Spirit World. I asked Kenneth to say his final words to his mother for now and to allow her to hug him (this is where the Spirit person pushes their energy forward so the sitter can actually feel a hug from their loved one). Then I asked the spirit to step aside and Kenneth to open his eyes and bring his awareness back into the room. When he opened his eyes, he lifted his head for the first time that evening. As he stood up, he had a broad smile on his face. I wanted to go over and give him a hug, but I sensed he mightn't want that, so I left it.

The transformation in Kenneth was remarkable, and plain for all to see. He now knew that although he had lost his mother on this physical earth plane, she was with him on a much higher level, from where, as she had said, she could guide him in a much more meaningful way than ever before. So in a loved one's passing, Spirit connection reminds us that we are not being robbed, but have been given the amazing gift of their continued love and guidance from the Spirit World to assist us in life's challenges. The transformational power of such knowledge for the person who has been bereaved cannot be underestimated and is wonderful to witness.

I will end this chapter with a reflection on what happens when a loved one passes over to the Spirit World, and how their presence there can be a huge source of comfort to us. I wrote this piece back in 2004, when I was composing a letter for a friend who had lost his mother and had asked Spirit for inspiration on what I could say to him. This reflection, *Togetherness*, is what Spirit gave to me.

TOGETHERNESS

It is always difficult to deal with the loss of a loved one. You should feel comforted to know that they are now in a better place. In the Spirit World where time does not exist, there is no pain, there is no fear, there is no suffering – there is only joy, happiness and peace.

You should feel comfort in knowing that your loved one is looking down on you, always guiding you, protecting you and your family, and helping you make decisions. They will always be with you. All you have to do is think about the times you laughed together, about the times you cried together, the good times and the bad times – and they are there with you.

In times of weakness, they will give you the strength to carry on; in times of sickness, they will be there to heal you; in times of happiness, they will be there to laugh with you. They may not be there in the physical, but you will feel their presence when you need them, helping you emotionally to get through the difficult times and rejoicing in the happy times.

You will always be together, never apart. You are always in their heart, as they are in yours. Look not on their passing as an end, but as a beginning for them in their new life, where someday in the future you will be reunited again.

5

THE HEALING POWER OF SPIRIT

> There is a light in this world, a healing spirit more powerful than any darkness we may encounter. We sometimes lose sight of this force when there is suffering, too much pain. Then suddenly, the spirit will emerge through the lives of ordinary people who hear a call and answer in extraordinary ways.
>
> *Mother Teresa*

We have seen the incredible emotional healing that communication with Spirit can bring to those who have been bereaved. But the power of Spirit to heal is not limited to emotional suffering, or just to those of us living on this earth plane. Connection with Spirit can bring about real physical healing, and contact between the two worlds can, as we will see, also be very beneficial for those who have already crossed over.

One remarkable story about healing, and the help that Spirit can come through with when we really need it, involves Katie, one of my young daughters. What started out as a fun family bank holiday weekend some years ago quickly turned into a situation of crisis, and my wife Linda and I found ourselves in one of the most frightening and helpless situations any parent can imagine. It was back in 2007, and Linda and I had decided to take our two older kids – Ben, then five years old, and Katie, who was almost three at the time – to London for the October bank holiday weekend. When we arrived back home in Celbridge late on the Monday evening the kids were exhausted, so we put them to bed. On the way home from the airport we had collected our other son, Darragh, from my parents' house: they had been looking after him for the weekend, as he was only six months old.

The next day, Katie went to Montessori school as usual and all seemed fine. That evening, however, we noticed that she seemed to be a bit out of sorts, but we just put it down to her being tired after our hectic weekend. Linda was to go into college later that evening, so it was just me at home with the kids. I'd put them to bed and all seemed okay, but at about ten o'clock, Katie woke up with a temperature and was sick a couple of times. I did my best to bring her temperature down, and put her into my bed beside me, watching her until she went back to sleep.

About an hour later, however, Katie woke again with the same symptoms – vomiting and a raised temperature. She was also complaining that the bedroom light was hurting her eyes. She had settled down again by the time Linda came in from college. On two occasions throughout the night, however, Katie woke again, both times with identical symptoms. Linda and I both thought it might be some bug that she had picked up on the plane on the way back from London.

The following day, a Wednesday, was Halloween. Linda felt there had been no improvement in Katie since the previous night, so she said she would take her to the doctor that morning. Our own doctor was on holiday, so Linda decided to take her to the doctor's surgery beside where we live. We were lucky on this occasion, as the day in question was an 'open surgery' day, which meant that you didn't need an advance appointment to get to see someone. I was in work that morning and so Linda said she would ring me and let me know how they got on at the surgery.

At about 10 a.m., Linda rang me to say Katie had

started to break out in a rash, so she had decided to set off immediately for the doctor's surgery. When she was finished there, she rang me in a panic. 'The doctor says we have to take Katie to the hospital immediately.'

'What's wrong with her?' I asked.

'She didn't say – just that we need to get her to hospital as soon as possible.'

I rang my mother and asked her to go over to our house, explaining that we had to take Katie to hospital and we needed someone to look after Darragh and Ben. I met Linda and Katie on the way – my sister had brought them to meet me. They transferred to my car and we set off for the hospital as quickly as possible – I was deliberately driving in bus lanes, actually hoping to get stopped by a policeman who would perhaps offer to escort us more quickly to the children's hospital in Crumlin. Katie has always been a bright and bubbly kid who loves drama and dance and is always bouncing around the place with a happy-go-lucky attitude. But that day, our little girl was not herself at all – she was pretty much lifeless, barely able to speak and her face was white and drawn.

When we got to the hospital, we went straight to the registration desk, telling the attendant what had happened and that the doctor had told us to get her to hospital immediately, without telling us why. A nurse came out and brought us into a cubicle there and then. As far as what happened next goes, all I can say is that it reminded me of a scene from the TV series *ER*. Suddenly, staff came from nowhere. There were at least three doctors and maybe four nurses, all rushing around, barking instructions to each other, such as, 'We need to get a line in!' and, 'I want bloods taken!' – as well as a lot of doctor-speak that we couldn't take in.

A senior nurse came over to Linda and me. 'What's going on?' I asked at once.

'We are not 100 per cent sure at the moment,' she replied, 'but Katie is showing all the signs and symptoms of meningitis. We are waiting for the bloods to come back, but in the meantime, we have started to administer the drugs for meningitis, as it is crucial to get these into her system as soon as possible.'

With that, a team of doctors and students suddenly crowded into Katie's cubicle. The consultant in charge came over and had a chat with us. He said that at this time of the year, it was unusual to get cases of meningitis. He asked permission for some of the students and other doctors to look at Katie's rash as the team worked on her, as this would be a rare opportunity for them to see such a rash in its early stages. We had no problem with this. Katie was still lying unresponsive and unmoving on the bed – her only reaction thus far had been to pull her arm away when the doctors tried to put a line in, so that they could take bloods and administer her drugs. 'Time is of the essence with this disease – it has to be caught early,' said the nurse who was keeping us updated.

Your child is lying lifeless on a bed, surrounded by doctors who are all working on her, doing many different things, and you are completely helpless. You can't do anything but watch and put your complete trust in the medical staff – you just have to hope that they know what they are doing and that they can help your child. So many things were running through my head at that moment, the main one being the same question, over and over again: 'Will she be okay – is she going to die?' Minutes felt like hours, as we continued to watch everything that was going on, completely helpless. I would never wish this experience on any parent. The worst part of all was not knowing what the outcome was going to be.

I don't know exactly how many hours had passed by the time the senior doctor came over to us, saying, 'We believe Katie has meningococcal septicaemia, and we have given her the drugs to counteract the bacterial infection. It's a time game now to see her reaction to the treatment.'

'What does that mean? A "time game"?' I asked, completely beside myself now. 'Are we going to lose her?'

The doctor said it was too early to say exactly what was going to happen and that we would just have to wait and see.

Meningococcal septicaemia is the often-fatal form of a disease that is not covered in the vaccinations that children get at the various stages of their young lives. The bacteria that cause meningococcal disease are common and live naturally at the back of the nose and throat. At any one time, one in ten of us carry the bacteria for weeks or months without ever knowing that they are there.[3] For the majority of people, this is harmless because, fortunately, most of us have natural resistance. The bacteria are so fragile that they cannot survive for more than a few moments outside the human body. For this reason, they are not very contagious: only a small fraction of people who are exposed to meningococcal bacteria will actually

3 Cartwright, K. A., Stuart, J. M., Jones D. M. & Noah, N. D., 'The Stonehouse Survey: Nasopharyngeal Carriage of Meningococcal and Neisseria Lactamica', *Epidemiology and Infection*, 99(3), 1987, pp. 591–601.

fall ill with the disease. The illness occurs when the bacteria break through the protective lining of the nose and throat, and enter the bloodstream. Once in the bloodstream, they multiply rapidly, doubling their numbers every thirty minutes. In some people the bacteria cross the blood/brain barrier, causing meningitis. In others, overwhelming septicaemia – or blood poisoning – occurs so quickly that there is no time for meningitis to develop.

When meningococcal bacteria invade your bloodstream, they produce poisons. This makes you feel ill and feverish, and the poisons begin to attack the lining of your blood vessels, so that these begin to leak. As blood fluids leak throughout the body, the smaller volume of blood that is left is not enough to carry oxygen to all parts of the body. Your lungs have to work harder, and in order to maintain circulation to your vital organs, your circulatory system reduces the blood supply to your hands and feet and the surface of your skin. This is how the symptoms of septicaemia develop, such as pale skin, cold hands and feet, and rapid breathing.[4] As blood leaks

4 Thompson, M. J., Ninis, N., Perera, R., Mayon-White. R., Phillips, C., Bailey, L., *et al.*, 'Clinical Recognition of Meningococcal Disease in Children and Adolescents', *The Lancet* 367, 2006, pp. 397–403.

into the surrounding tissues, this shows up as the typical meningococcal rash, which does not disappear whenever pressure is applied to the skin.

The doctors told us that it was very lucky that we got Katie to hospital when we did: they said that if it had been even a few hours later, things would have been very different. Katie was transferred to the Intensive Care Unit. Now it was indeed just a waiting game – there was nothing else we could do.

Well, there was something I could do. I started to contact all the healers I knew from around the world – by text, e-mail and phone – and asked them to send healing energy to Katie. Then I sat by her bed, where she lay attached to a multitude of machines with flashing lights and beeping sounds, monitoring her every movement, heartbeat and breath. I put one of my hands on Katie's stomach and the other on her hand, called on all my angel guides and loved ones from the Spirit World and sat there channelling all the energy from them into Katie. When I do healing work (placing my hands either on or above the body and channelling Spirit through my body to provide healing to the individual receiving the healing), my hands can get extremely hot, especially in the centre of my palms, an area which is known as the healing circle. My hands now were on fire. I sat there for hours, just looking at my little girl, continually calling in all the help from the Spirit World that I could.

By this time, it was about eleven o'clock at night – we had already been in the hospital for ten hours. Linda suggested that I go home to update our families, who had all congregated in our house. I could also fetch some clothes and various things for Katie and Linda, who had been allocated a bed in the 'family tower' in the hospital, an area for parents who want to stay overnight with their sick children. So I gave Katie a kiss – she was still in a comatose state – and headed home.

When I got back to the house, Ben, our older son, was still up: it was Halloween night and he had been out trick-or-treating in the neighbourhood with his granddad and cousins. As soon as I arrived, Ben ran to me and jumped into my arms. I filled up with tears, trying not to let him see me cry. The hug of your child is so comforting, pure and healing at such a time. He asked how Katie was. I told him she was in hospital and that the doctors were making her better. 'Will she be home tomorrow?' was his next question.

'We will ask the doctors when she can come home – okay?' was all I could manage in reply.

'Okay,' said Ben. He showed me the bag of treats he had got for his Halloween efforts, and said he had a bag for Katie too and would bring them in to her the next day.

When I went back to the hospital the following morning, Katie's condition had improved – but she was still critical. I sat with her and again called in all the guides, spirits and loved ones I could think of, asking them to send healing to Katie, and I channelled this healing energy to her. When the doctors came around to give us an update, they said it was a good sign that her condition hadn't deteriorated any further – although it hadn't improved either.

In the early afternoon of that day, Katie finally opened her eyes and, frightened and confused by her surroundings, started to cry. Linda and I went to comfort her. She was still very weak. She kept trying to pull out the line in her arm, so we explained to her that this was 'Freddy': it was her job to mind him, and the nurses had to feed him every so often. Being the really motherly type, Katie thought it was great that she had to mind this thing in her arm called Freddy, and that she had such a thing and we didn't!

Over the next few hours, Katie's condition rapidly improved. The nurses decided that she was well enough to be transferred to a ward. While we were waiting for a porter to wheel the bed down, Katie asked if she could get up and she came to sit in my arms. So I said to the nurse, 'I can carry Katie down to the ward like this.'

In amazement, the nurse replied: 'We have never had a child carried out of Intensive Care – this is a first!' Normally, she said, it was at least three days before a child with Katie's condition could be moved out of the high-dependency unit – and even then, no child had ever been alert enough to be carried out by a parent. She added that everyone on the ward was amazed at the rate of recovery they had witnessed in Katie. Even the doctors were astonished at how quickly she had turned around. All I can attribute this miraculous improvement to was the quick and expert work of the medical team, as well as – undeniably, as far as I am concerned – the healing powers of the Spirit World I had called upon, and the positive energies the healers around the world had been sending to Katie. I believe that it was in Katie's sacred contract that it was not her time to pass, therefore the healing power of the Spirit World helped her get through her ordeal.

Strangely enough, earlier that year – in March 2007 – I had been listening one day to a Dublin radio station that was running a 'Care for Kids radio-a-thon', to raise money for the children's hospitals in Dublin. I remember saying to Linda, 'We should donate money to the children's hospitals – you never know when we might need them.' So we made a donation then – only to find ourselves, some months later, in desperate need of their services for one of our own children! To this day, I am a big advocate of fund-raising for children's hospitals, and as of February 2014 I have raised over €8,000 for the Children's Hospital in Crumlin – the one where Katie was treated. Having been through the awful ordeal of not knowing whether one of our children was going to live or die, I am more determined than ever to keep up my fund-raising efforts. All funds I raise go to the Oncology Unit at the hospital.

~

As I said earlier, it's not only those of us in this world who can benefit from the healing power of Spirit connection. Healing is not a one-way street, and spirits too can benefit from the positive energy which connection can bring. This is where the phenomenon of 'Spirit rescue' comes into play. As a working medium, I have been called upon to facilitate Spirit rescues on many occasions.

In the simplest terms, a 'rescue' may be required where a spirit has not, for whatever reason, been able to make the full transition to the Spirit World. Such spirits are referred to as 'earthbound' because, having been unable to cross successfully at the moment of passing, they remain in this earthly dimension and bound to the physical world, even though they themselves no longer have any physical form. The reasons why they have been unable or unwilling to transition successfully are many and complex, and are not connected to the person's way of crossing over or what they were like here on the physical plane.

When called upon to do so, a medium can help an earthbound spirit to make the transition to the Spirit World, making the connection with the Spirit guides and helpers who have been assigned to assist that spirit. Earthbound spirits are unaware of the presence of these guides meant to help them until they are pointed out to them during the course of the rescue. Not all earthbound spirits are amenable to rescue, and this is something that can never be forced. Some are perfectly happy with their situation and want to continue their existence on this earth plane. Many, however, will gladly accept an intervention to help them move on to the Spirit World. Earthbound spirits, particularly those who are troubled by the situation they find themselves in, will make their presence felt in a number of ways, e.g. knocking, banging, giving the feeling of someone being there, and it is in such circumstances that people will often solicit the intervention of a medium.

Several years ago, I got a phone call from a man who said he needed my help as a matter of urgency. He explained that he and his family were having trouble with Spirit activity in their home and asked if I would be able to come to investigate what was going on and try to bring some calm back into the house. He said that he had been experiencing different things: hearing noises, such as knocking and banging and the sound of footsteps, and being woken up at night by what he assumed were spirits, pulling at his bedclothes. I agreed to meet him and see what I could do to help.

I drove to this guy's local village to meet him. When I pulled up, neither of us got out of our cars – I followed him in my car to his home, a few minutes' drive from the village. The place was a really nice-looking, detached house, with quite a bit of land around it. I followed the owner into the driveway and parked. As I stepped out of my car, I was seized by a fit of uncontrollable coughing. The man was a bit unnerved and kept asking if I was okay. I fetched a bottle of water from my car. After a couple of minutes and about a litre of water, I was finally able to talk to this guy, who must have been thinking: *What on earth have I got myself into?*

'Are you okay?' he repeated.

'Yes, I am fine, thanks,' I replied. 'I'm just picking up a Spirit energy – it is very strong. I have to tell you that a young man passed here through asphyxiation. I need to contact someone called Joe.'

'Joe's my neighbour,' he said. 'Where exactly are you picking up this energy?'

'The top, far window of your house,' I said, pointing to the furthest window from where I was standing – up on the second floor of the house.

'That's where we are getting most of the activity,' the man replied in amazement. 'That's unreal!'

I continued to tell him about the young man. 'I see him playing football,' I said.

'My neighbour Joe's son hung himself on the land where our house is a number of years ago,' he said finally. 'He used to play football with the other children around here, in the field our house is built on.' As he spoke, he had a look of complete bewilderment on his face. He didn't seem able to take in the information I had just given him and kept repeating, 'That's unreal!'

We went into the house, where I was introduced to the man's wife, mother, brother and sisters: all were waiting patiently to hear what I had to say and what my investigation might uncover. I went straight upstairs and into the room I had pointed to earlier and it was like an icebox – absolutely freezing. I went over to one of the corners. 'Here is where the activity is,' I said.

'Yes!' the guy replied. 'This is where everything happens.'

So I started to connect with the young man's energy and I began to attempt a 'scene rescue', to help him cross over to the Spirit World. A scene rescue typically involves mentally reframing an earthbound spirit's environment, or 'scene', to one in which they feel comfortable and safe. So if, for example, they perceive themselves as being somewhere dark and oppressive, you begin, by visualisation, to gradually shift this into something brighter and better. In a sense, it doesn't matter what the alternative scene you create mentally for them is – it might be a beautiful garden, a tranquil countryside scene or a sunny beach. The important thing is that you are trying to shift their focus onto something better and more positive than their current predicament. A medium can elicit help in working out what scene might best appeal to the spirit in question by calling upon their Spirit guides.

As I did these things and channelled positive energy towards the young man in that cold, dark bedroom, a tunnel of light to the Spirit World (which we refer to as a 'portal') opened up, and two women stepped into view. 'This young man's mother and grandmother are both coming forward, to help him cross over,' I explained to the owner of the house. 'His mother is not that long crossed – she passed just about two years ago, from a cancerous condition.'

Again the man was amazed. 'That's unbelievable,' he said. 'How you are getting all of this information?'

As I was doing the rescue, I could sense another Spirit gentleman in the room with us. He jumped into the light with the young man, his mother and grandmother, and the portal closed, signifying that the Spirit rescue of the young man had been successful. But then I saw the same older gentleman reappearing from Spirit side. As he started to move out of the room, I decided to follow him, into a bedroom on the other side of the house. 'I need to go in here now,' I told the house owner. So we went into the room and the Spirit man was standing in the corner. 'There is activity in this room too,' I explained. 'There is a father figure here – someone who passed from a heart condition, quickly and suddenly.'

'I sometimes sleep in this room, when the children take over our bed,' the owner said. 'I often feel something in here: a presence sitting on the bed and tugging at my bedclothes. And even though it sounds mad, I am not scared by it – I am intrigued but don't feel threatened by it.'

'This really feels to me like the energy of a father figure and someone I need to connect with,' I continued.

'My dad had cancer,' he said.

'No, this gentleman passed from a heart condition – I can feel it in my chest,' I told him.

Then we went back down to the kitchen, where the family were all eagerly waiting to hear what we had found and experienced. The Spirit gentleman came with us. The house owner started to tell his family about what had happened and about the evidence and information that I had been able to bring through – including the detail I had given about the father figure having a heart condition.

'That's your dad!' the owner's mother said at once. 'He's around all the time. Your dad had cancer, but he died of a heart attack – he had just come back from the hospital after a check-up and he sat down on the stairs, only to have a massive heart attack and die instantly.'

'I thought it was the cancer that he had died from!' her son said.

This was another instance where the person who is getting the reading doesn't know the full history of what has happened. The Spirit gentleman had come forward very clearly, giving me the correct information, but the sitter in this case – the owner of the house – didn't have the knowledge to be able to verify it; this happens quite a lot.

The man started to cry, saying, 'That's my dad around me! I felt so safe with him there!'

I then asked the family if they would like to feel the energy of the Spirit gentleman. They all jumped at the chance, and one by one they came forward to be connected with their loved one's energy. More than one of them became quite tearful as they felt his energy blend with theirs and, as he hugged each of them, they could feel the sensation around their necks.

When it came to the turn of the Spirit gentleman's wife, the mother of the owner of the house, I asked her if she wished to feel his energy. 'I feel it all the time,' she replied. 'He lies in the bed beside me at night – I can feel him and sense when he is with me.'

All of the family were amazed.

'You never told us any of this, Mam!' they said.

'Sure, you would just have thought I was mad,' she told them.

The older Spirit gentleman was able to give a lot of information about himself – things he would have said, his personality, his memories – and all of these details were acknowledged by his family. Joe the neighbour – the father of the young Spirit gentleman I had helped to rescue – was also able to later verify the information I had been able to bring through from his son.

It was a very touching experience that day to be able to witness the young Spirit gentleman being greeted and brought into the light by his mother and grandmother, his Spirit guides. There was a great sense of resolution and peace afterwards. It was also very moving to see a connection of great love between the house owner's father and his wife, daughters and the extended family. It felt as if a lot of good things had been achieved by Spirit that day, and an important sense of healing had been given to both the Spirit loved ones and their earthly families.

6

IT'S NOT A GIFT, IT'S AN ABILITY: TUNING IN TO THE SPIRIT WORLD

> Of mediumship there are many grades, one of the simplest forms being the capacity to receive an impression or automatic writing, under peaceful conditions, in an ordinary state …
>
> *Oliver Joseph Lodge*

When I hear people use the word 'gift' in connection to mediumship and communication with Spirit, I cringe. I don't like the word 'gift' in this context – it suggests that only a chosen few have been given the innate ability to connect with Spirit; that it is only those who are in some way 'special' who can do such things. It is my belief, however, that mediumship and connecting with the Spirit

World is an ability, not a gift – it is something which we all have and which each one of us can further develop, should we wish to do so.

Everyone can pick up a paintbrush and paint a picture of some description. There are some people who have developed their artistic skills and can paint a portrait or a landscape scene, while others may just be able to paint a simple representation. It is the same with mediumship: some people have developed their abilities to connect with Spirit more fully than others. As in the case of any other ability or skill, there are perhaps some who have a greater natural aptitude for mediumship than others – but all of us have the basic ability to communicate with the Spirit World, and it is an ability that can be enhanced through practice and work.

It was at an evening of mediumship in the Civic Theatre, Tallaght, in 2009 that I fully realised the extent to which every single one of us has mediumistic abilities to some degree. At my mediumship circle and various development classes, I had begun to introduce a new element when doing readings with individuals – this consisted of me asking sitters if they wanted to be able to feel at first-hand the energy of their Spirit loved one. If the person was agreeable, I would have them stay in the sitter's chair and then I would attempt to channel the energy of the communicator to them, while telling the rest of the circle or class members to watch carefully for any changes in the sitter's face and demeanour. This had been very successful for many of those in my circle, but it was at the public event in Tallaght that I decided for the first time to see if someone who *wasn't* working actively on developing their abilities as a medium could feel the closeness of Spirit and allow the energy of a Spirit loved one into their physical body.

In the interval at that demonstration, a lady came up to me with a photograph of her son who had passed. She asked me if I could connect to a picture and get a communication in this way from a Spirit loved one. This is known as 'psychometry', which is where you connect to an object belonging to a person and from this you are able to channel information and Spirit communication relating to that individual. Although I had done this before in the more intimate 'closed' setting of circle readings, it was not something I had planned to do as part of a public demonstration. But this lady was pleading with me, as she had lost her young son and wanted desperately to make a connection with him. So, once I was back on stage after the interval, I told the audience that I was going to try to connect with a photograph that I had just been given.

I held the photograph of the little boy to my chest, calling upon his energy to connect with me. Instantly the name Paddy came to me, and I started to say the name over and over, 'Paddy – Paddy – Paddy …'

'Yes!' the lady exclaimed. 'That's my little boy!' A lot of the information I was able to channel thereafter was a blur for Paddy's mother, as she got caught up in the emotion of the moment, while her friend tried to console her. Paddy described the circumstances in which he had passed, causing me to feel the sensations directly as a way of explaining how he had felt at the time. He then showed me a little toy, which was like a walking duck: as you pulled it along the floor, the duck's legs rotated up and around in the air, like a Ferris wheel. When his mother said she didn't understand this reference, her friend spoke up, reminding her, 'That was the only Christmas present Paddy opened himself – the little duck that you pull along.' Sadly Paddy had been too ill that Christmas Day to be able to open any of his other presents himself. His mother cried even more at the memory.

Wanting very much to console her, I asked if she would like to feel her son's energy for herself. 'Yes!' she cried. 'Yes!' So she came up onto the stage and I got a chair, motioning for her to sit down and relax. I began by asking her if she gave permission for her son to enter her physical field of energy. 'Yes,' she nodded. With that, the little boy literally jumped up onto her lap and into her energy! Instantaneously, his mother stopped crying and became completely composed. Her face relaxed and her whole body was calm. Her hands, which had previously been shaking, became still.

I asked Paddy to push his energy forward into his mother's fingers. He started to focus on his mother's right hand, which began to lift up off her lap, little by little. As I witnessed this phenomenon – which is the only word I can use to describe it – my heart was racing. If this could happen for someone who was not actively developing their mediumship and exploring the world of Spirit, then it was within everyone's reach! This was a moment of epiphany for me, when I fully realised that all of us – each and every one – has the power to access the world of Spirit. We may each have different levels of ability and of desire to do so, but essentially it is something we can all do.

At this point I got Paddy to give his mother a hug and then asked him to separate his energy from hers.

She opened her eyes, not really sure of exactly what had happened, except for the fact that she knew for certain that her son had connected with her. She had felt him, smelled his familiar smell and been hugged by him, feeling the sensation of him squeezing on her neck in the way he had always done.

I felt more than a little overwhelmed by all of this myself, as did a lot of the audience. It was then that I realised how important it was for me to bring this experience to others around the country and show them that they too could connect strongly and feel the presence of their Spirit loved ones. I have always experienced, by the way, a very strong sense of connection to the energy of children who have passed over. I tend to find that those who have only had a short time physically here on earth can bring through some amazing evidence and a very intense sense of connection. People lose loved ones to the Spirit World all the time, but to lose a child is a very different thing, as you never expect that your children will pass before you.

As babies and young children, we are very connected and open to Spirit, but somehow the majority of us lose our awareness of this connection through the general run of physical life, as well as the conditioning that usually begins in early childhood. By conditioning, I am thinking of the system of beliefs which most children are introduced to from their earliest school years and which is imposed by religion and generally by society itself: the system of beliefs that includes very cut-and-dried ideas about what is right and what is wrong, what spiritual beliefs are acceptable or otherwise, and so on. Irish children are told early in life that any kind of connection with the world of Spirit outside the context of the traditional church is wrong, and even, to quote the words used by a minister I once had a tough exchange with, 'the work of the Devil'. So it is hardly surprising that, very early on in life, many of us tune out communications from Spirit and rule out the idea of seeking connection with the Spirit World.

Most people have a turning point in their lives, when they reconnect with Spirit. Very often, as in my own case with the passing of my Uncle Richard, that moment can be an event such as the loss of a loved one, as a result of which someone will begin to look for answers and think about developing their mediumship abilities in a quest to reconnect with those who are no longer in their lives. Here are some responses from people I spoke to for the book, on the issue of how a loved one's death changed their perspective:

The Spirit World was always something I wondered about but I wasn't sure it truly existed until my father passed away suddenly, fourteen years ago. We were devastated, as people are by a sudden death. His first little trick after passing was to divert our home phone to his mobile, which was still with his belongings in the morgue.

We didn't know what his cause of death was, and so had to wait for toxicology results after his post-mortem. Before this, however, my father came to me in a dream one night. In the dream, I could see his body lying on the left side on the floor, with his feet near the door – suddenly, his voice came from behind my right shoulder (even though his body was in front of me) and he explained gas leaking from the gas heater was what had killed him. In my dream, water flowed from the heater and soaked into his head – this was obviously symbolising what had happened. In the dream, he also gave me messages for the family and said the goodbyes he never got a chance to say before his death.

When the day of his inquest came around, I told my uncles about the dream I had had, but they just laughed at me. But everything that we were told at the inquest in fact was exactly as I had dreamed it to be. And that was why I became a medium – because it was proven to me that our spirit lives on after the death of our physical body.

~

I have had communication with my nan since she passed. Exactly one week after she died, we held her funeral and that same night when I was in bed, I felt this strong mass of energy take over my body – it was very intense. At the same time, to the left of me I saw this vortex opening, with a beautiful, bright green, swirling light shining from it. Then I heard my nan's voice, as clear as day, calling my name: it was distant, but it was definitely her. She said my name twice, then I felt her energy fade [again]. I will treasure that moment forever: it was a beautiful gift from her and I am so blessed to have received it! To this day, I often feel her visiting me. Life doesn't end – our passed loved ones are still around us, they are just out of sight to most other people.

~

When my dad passed over sixteen years ago, I was devastated … but also nervous, in case he came to visit me. One night just after he passed, I was asleep in bed and was woken by a warm breeze blowing on my face. I just knew it was my dad and I was not one bit nervous. I have had messages from him, about things only he knew … He has visited me in dreams, he also told a medium that I was going to be a grandma, before even my daughter knew – he gave the right date and time. It has helped me so much to know that my dad is still living on and that one day I will see him once more.

I have also felt my husband around me and have seen him in a vision while I was awake – I was just lying in bed and he suddenly appeared. It even happened when my dog died – he used to sleep at the side of our bed, and for about three weeks after his death, a little light kept floating above that side of the bed …

While the passing of a loved one is one of the most common catalysts in the search for evidence of the Spirit World, there are any number of life events that can kick off a spiritual reawakening. Many people may have already been receiving communications from Spirit without being aware of it.

Have you ever been driving in your car, only to suddenly be aware of a strong smell of perfume – but you are not wearing that perfume yourself and there is no one else in the car with you? Or there are those random thoughts that come into your head without explanation or logic. Or those periods in your life when, each time you turn on the radio, a particular song always seems to be playing, one that is associated with a loved one who has passed. Perhaps you notice a number sequence recurring in different contexts, or are struck by the particular way in which people may say or phrase things. Each of these occurrences may be an instance of communication from Spirit, and the more you become aware of this as a possibility, the more you will start to see patterns building up and daily examples of synchronicity which seem too striking to be merely coincidences.

So, how can we go about developing our receptiveness to Spirit communication and indeed our own ability to connect? *Awareness* is the first and key principle of Spirit communication: the awareness that Spirit is around us, looking to connect with us. So often we doubt the voices we hear, the thoughts we have, the images we see, or any of the other signs we are being given, because we think it is all in our imagination. But so often, that's not the case at all.

In order to perceive the physical world around us, we use our five physical senses – sight, hearing, smell, touch and taste. Correspondingly, in perceiving and connecting with the Spirit World, we also depend on a number of different senses to help us: these are the 'clair' senses, the same five basic human senses – except that they are used on a mediumship level instead. The five 'clair' senses of mediumship are:

- *Clairvoyance* (or 'clear seeing') – this is the ability to see Spirit, often in the mind's eye. Spirit may bring through objects, symbols or scenes as a means of communicating a specific message: these may appear as pictures or stills, or as movie footage in a medium's 'mind's eye'. Other mediums may see Spirit in a physical form, as if it was actually present.

- *Clairaudience* (or 'clear hearing') – this is the ability to perceive Spirit and Spirit communications through hearing or thoughts. Some mediums – myself included – hear the voices or thoughts of Spirit as their own 'mind's voice', i.e. as part of that constant internal monologue we all have, which is our own train of thought. Other mediums may hear Spirit as though they are listening to an external person talking to them.

- *Clairsentience* (or 'clear feeling') – the ability to perceive messages from Spirit through feelings or sensations. A medium may be able to feel the emotions of Spirit, or the physical feelings or sensations a spirit might have experienced around the time of their death. For example, through clairsentience, I have felt chest pains, pressure on my heart, stomach pains and so on. In other cases, I have felt intense emotions ranging from joy and love, to misery and despair.

- *Clairambience* ('clear smelling') – the ability to perceive communication from Spirit through smell. A medium may pick up a smell – a perfume or aftershave, for example – specifically associated with someone while they were on the earth plane.

- *Clairalience* ('clear tasting') – the ability to perceive communication from Spirit through taste. As with clairambience, a medium experiences distinctive tastes which may be associated with the Spirit communicator, or which may help to convey a particular message.

As with our regular five senses, it is the case with the 'clair' senses too that most people tend to have one or two dominant senses that they use most commonly, while the others senses remain secondary. To help illustrate this, I asked a number of people who have recently started to reconnect with Spirit and develop their mediumship abilities, which of the senses they find themselves using most when trying to pick up a communication. Here are some of the replies I received:

> My connections are mostly clairaudient and clairsentient, as I hear and feel more than see.

~

I use clairvoyance. I see things when I close my eyes. Good thing about it – I don't have to pay for a TV licence!

~

I see in my mind's eye, not with my actual eyes … Both my eight-year-old son and I dream and 'travel' (astrally) too, so which 'clair' sense do you count that as? I hear as well – but not like someone in the room talking to me – I hear in my head …

~

I feel and sense presence. And I also have heard and felt presence. I sometimes get pre-warning in a dream of something that is going to happen.

~

I use them all at some stage, but clairsentience seems to come easiest, and then clairaudience and clairvoyance … Sometimes I just know something. I communicate daily with a spirit, and it's just like 'thought talking'. I don't actually hear a voice, but now and then I get a funny sensation – like bubbling or butterflies [in my ears]. If you try too hard to hear, it doesn't come easily. Really hard sometimes to work out what is your [own] mind and what is Spirit …

Particularly fascinating in terms of using the 'clair' senses is this account from Jen Loring, who draws 'Spirit portraits' when she connects with the Spirit World, and brings through a lot of concrete details relating to the Spirit person in each portrait, which she writes in note form beside her drawings:

> I seem to get all the senses. I use them in my Spirit portraits. To start with, I say a prayer for protection. From there, I would have to say the drawings are similar in a way to automatic writing. I've never actually done automatic writing but have seen others do it. I start off drawing the eyes and then the picture develops on its own. At the same time, I hear or sense thoughts, which I write down next to the drawings. I have heard laughter at times. I do see Spirit mostly in my mind's eye, but hardly ever in the context of the portraits. A quarter of [the portraits] have been claimed. One of them, a man from South Africa, was claimed by a woman at the church I go to. Some months later, she brought in a photo of him – the likeness gave me goose bumps …

You can see Jen's portraits on her Facebook page, *Spirit Portraits and the Information with Them.*

So, if you are looking for concrete, practical ways

through which you can begin to heighten your awareness to all things spiritual, here are some suggestions to bear in mind:

- Key to any development is, above all, to learn to trust the information and communications you are being sent by Spirit.
- Practise meditation to calm the mind, so that you can be open and receptive to communications from Spirit.
- Get involved in a circle facilitated by a reputable, working medium.
- Try to develop as many of the 'clair' senses as possible, and at least the two main senses which seem to be dominant for you.
- Practise doing readings for circle members within the relatively safe and intimate environment of a mediumship development circle.
- Aim to become aware of and build up your references of the way Spirit tends to communicate with you: for example, are the images and words you have been given literal or symbolic references, and so on.

The second point above, about meditation as a means of calming the mind, is one of the most important ways you can begin to heighten your awareness. It makes sense that, when we connect to Spirit and try to establish communication, we need to have our minds clear of the normal, everyday stuff that, for most of us, tends to dominate our inner monologue: *I have to get petrol for the car; I have to get groceries; I have to run this errand; I have to complete that task,* etc. – these are the types of thoughts that constantly fill our minds on a daily basis.

The key to any form of meditation is to allow the mind to become as still and quiet as possible. A lot of people find this one of the hardest things to achieve. Yet the stiller the mind, the easier it is to connect with Spirit and sense when it is trying to connect with you. This is why so many of us will have found ourselves being woken up between 3 and 4 a.m. by a presence or by a voice or even a vivid, intense dream. It is during this time of the twenty-four-hour cycle that our minds are at their quietest, and so this is when Spirit will most readily try to connect with us. That is not to say that this is the only time that Spirit will communicate with us. It is ready to communicate with us at any time and all the time, but if our minds are overloaded and preoccupied with day-to-day matters, we can miss these attempts to connect. Later I will share with you one of the most effective meditation exercises

I have used within my circles and classes – and one that was given to me directly by Spirit.

Spirit will communicate with you most effectively when the conditions are right. Your frame of mind is very important – and not only in the sense of being calm and cleared of intrusive, everyday thoughts. The importance of creating the right conditions for Spirit to come through was brought home to me very clearly on one particular occasion a few years ago and it is an insight from Spirit I was very grateful for – even if it caused me some difficulties at the time.

On this occasion, I had been asked to visit a house where a group of eight women had gathered in the hope of each getting a one-to-one reading with me. I managed to find the house without any problems and when I arrived the group wasted no time in installing me in a room where I would be able to see each one of them for an individual reading. As soon as I was settled in, I called the first lady in and began a reading for her. All went well, and one after another, three more of the women came into the room. Each time I was able to connect with their loved ones in the Spirit World and bring good evidence through, which each sitter seemed very pleased with.

I was halfway through my session at the house – I

had completed four readings and there were four more ladies waiting their turn, when the fifth sitter came in to me. I tried to establish a connection for her; I got a complete blank. I pushed Spirit and kept pushing, but absolutely nothing was coming through for me. After a while, I asked the lady if she wanted to let the next sitter come in, telling her that I would come back to her again – if she could wait for another hour or so, I would try again to make a connection at that stage.

So the next lady came in and sat down before me. But the same thing happened this time too – nothing was coming through to me for her either. I couldn't understand it, and kept saying to those in the Spirit World, 'Why have you guys stopped?' I was genuinely puzzled. I had no luck with the next sitter and, by the time I came to the eighth and last lady, it was hardly a surprise that, yet again, Spirit was completely unresponsive. Feeling frustrated and a little baffled, I had to tell the host of the night that I couldn't finish off the readings – that I was sorry but it seemed that I wasn't going to be able to get any further information for the sitters that evening.

It was only as I was driving home that I suddenly realised what had been happening. The Spirit World vibration is a much higher vibration than the earth/physical realm. The best way to explain it is to use the analogy of radio stations on different frequencies. Mediums have to raise their vibration and Spirit has to bring its vibration down to match theirs for a communication to happen, so it takes a lot of energy for Spirit to connect with us from the other side and give us messages. The second group of women had been drinking a fair amount of alcohol while they waited their turn for the readings, and I guessed that this was the reason they hadn't got any connections – unlike the first four women, who had had relatively little to drink before their readings. When I told other mediums about the evening and my theory about the part played by alcohol, quite a few of them reported similar experiences – that when alcohol was involved, they had found it harder to get communications from the Spirit World. It makes sense of course – if you are under the influence of alcohol, you do not relate to things as you normally do and this in turn will affect the way in which you connect with Spirit. Also, depending on how intoxicated a person is, they may not remember any of the information given to them from Spirit, or be able to properly interpret anything that does come through. It is clear then that spirits and the Spirit World do not mix!

In my view, for someone to go to a reading under the

influence of alcohol shows disrespect for Spirit in any case, as it does take a lot of effort from the Spirit side for a communication to happen at all. It is hardly surprising that Spirit does not respond in these circumstances.

I would now like to share with you a powerful meditation that I use in my circle and mediumship classes when helping people to create the right state of mind for connecting with Spirit. This meditation was given to me directly from Spirit. I was lying in bed one evening, reading a book, when I sensed that I should get a pen and paper. Not knowing what was going to happen or what I was going to be given, I felt intrigued and energised. I fetched a pen and a piece of paper, and over the next forty minutes Spirit gave me words, which I wrote down as quickly as they came into my mind. Just as some years previously, when I had been given the piece 'Togetherness', which I shared with you in an earlier chapter, here too the words flowed quickly and easily, with no effort on my part.

Here are the words that were given to me:

> Close your eyes, allow your mind to slow down, to quieten, let your daily thoughts gently float away. Notice your breathing and take a long, deep breath, allowing the air

to fill your lungs. Release all your worries and fears as you exhale, continuing with the rhythmic flow of your breathing, each time releasing all your worries and fears on the exhalation.

Bring your attention now to your crown chakra, at the top of your head. Notice the white light connection coming from your crown chakra, connecting you to the Source – the Spirit realm.

Now visualise a control panel that manages your connection to the Source energy. Your connection is set to 'low'. Press the auto-increase button. This will raise your energy connection to a more powerful vibration and the energy will slowly get stronger and stronger. There are four settings on the connection control dial, from low to highest. The dial is now at 'medium'. Feel the energy getting stronger and stronger, and the light getting brighter and brighter. The dial is now at 'high', as the energy gets stronger still, and the light brighter and brighter. The dial is still moving and is now nearly at the 'highest' level. Your mind is calm and quiet. As the energy is getting stronger and stronger, and the light brighter and brighter, the dial has reached its 'highest' setting. You are sensitive to the change in energy in you and around you. You feel lighter and in complete control of your energy.

Now you are standing outside a lift that only has one button. Press the button and the doors open. You are greeted by one of your Spirit guides – you say hello and you embrace each other. Get into the lift and press the 'up' arrow on the control panel inside. The doors close and the lift starts slowly to ascend. As the lift ascends, it gathers more and more speed, raising your vibration and further increasing your connection to Spirit, as you go up and up. The floor counter above the inside door shows the numbers 1 to 20, the arrow is now moving from 1 to 2 to 3, 4, 5, 6, 7, 8, 9 and 10 ... Your energy vibration is getting higher and higher, as the floors pass by – 11, 12, 13, 14 ... The vibration is getting higher and higher – 15, 16, 17, 18 – and still higher and higher – 19, 20! The lift stops and the doors open. You have reached the Spirit realm: you have arrived home.

Notice your surroundings and your environment. The air is clean and crisp to breathe. There is a sense of calm, a sense of peace, a sense of knowing, a sense of being [yourself]. Your Spirit guide brings you along a winding pathway through an evergreen forest of tall trees. The smell of pine hits your nostrils, the smell of wood, the smell of nature. You can hear the sound of a running stream, as water flows over the smooth rock on the stream bed. You arrive at a large clearing in the forest. There is a campfire burning, brightly and tall, with glowing embers of orange and red. There are a lot of people gathered at the campfire, all dressed in robe-like garments, all with a sense of calm, a sense of peace, a sense of knowing, a sense of being.

To the left of the campfire there is a reserved area, which has been set aside for you: this is where you are going to meet one of your loved ones. This place is familiar to you, as if you have been here before ... You have a sense of calm, a sense of peace, a sense of knowing, a sense of being. As you sit down on one of the large rock chairs, your Spirit guide leaves you and disappears into the crowd. You sit alone and contemplate the stillness of the moment. You look towards the crowd by the campfire.

Now the crowd parts and one of the congregation steps forward and starts to walk towards you, their face becoming clearer and clearer as they get closer and closer. You recognise the face and rise to your feet, hugging and embracing your loved one. Their appearance and energy appears the same as it was when they were on the earth plane. You both sit down and catch up on things that have been happening.

You ask your loved one a question. They offer guidance on your question, stating that it is up to you to make the decision. They can only give you guidance: you must be responsible for your own choices and decisions.

Now your loved one lifts up a gold-wrapped present for you, which has a big red bow on the top, and asks you to open the present. Acknowledge the present, its meaning or purpose. Thank your loved one for the gift.

Your Spirit guide returns from the crowd and you

finish your conversation with your loved one. Give them a hug and say your goodbyes for now. Remember, your loved one hasn't gone anywhere, they have just moved on.

Your Spirit guide brings you back along the winding pathway, through the evergreen forest of tall trees. You hear the sound of the water as it flows over the smooth rocks along the stream bed. You smell nature, you smell wood, you smell the pine, as you go back towards the lift.

You enter the lift and press the 'down' button. The doors close and the lift starts to descend – 20, 19, 18, 17, 16, 15 … The energy vibration is getting lower and lower. Down, down you go – 14, 13 … Down, down – 12, 11, 10 … lower and lower – 9, 8 … Down, down – 7, 6, 5, 4, 3 … Down, down – 2, 1. The lift comes to a stop, you thank your Spirit guide for escorting you on the journey, you embrace and say your goodbyes for now, as you step out of the lift.

You are now back on the earth plane. You are aware that you are back in the room, you sense the environment you are in and you smell the atmosphere around you in the room.

Now visualise the control panel that manages your connection to the Source energy. Your connection is set to 'highest'. Press the auto-decrease button. This will bring your energy connection to a lower vibration. The energy will slowly get weaker and weaker. The strong connection from your crown chakra to the Source eases. You see the dial on the control panel moving from 'highest' to 'high', as the bright light starts to dim and the connection gets weaker and weaker. The dial turns to 'medium', the light continues to dim and the energy connection continues to get weaker and weaker. The connection and the white light are now on the 'low' setting.

Visualise roots growing from the soles of your feet, going deep, deep, deep down into the centre of the earth. You will see a large crystal in the centre of the earth with your name on it. Wrap your roots firmly around the crystal, feel your connection to Mother Earth and feel the pull towards her centre, grounding you and your spirit in your physical body. Gently start to move your feet, your fingers, gently open your eyes and be fully present in the room.

Remember, you can visit the Spirit World at any time. Contemplate and acknowledge what you have experienced during the meditation.

I was delighted with this meditation I had received and when I asked Spirit what name I should give it, these words came to mind: 'Going Home – The Reunion'. I decided that I would share the piece with my circle groups and wasted no time in doing so, bringing it with me to the next circle meeting. My circle members found it very easy to follow and many of them went very deeply into the meditation, with some getting quite emotional.

Since then I have often drawn on the 'Going Home' meditation in my work with classes and circles. People have told me that they never get the same thing twice from it – each journey is different. There are certain things which are constant, however: people feel their energy vibration rising as they go up in the lift; the experience of being in the Spirit World feels very real to them; and when they meet their loved ones, it is as if they are talking to them one-on-one in the physical world.

Since the 'Going Home' meditation proved so effective with my groups, I decided to look into getting it produced as a CD. This proved to be a very interesting journey in itself, in which synchronicity played an important part – clear proof to me that I had the backing of Spirit in my efforts. I was able to find a fantastic composer and collaborative partner in David Beaupré, who set the meditation to music for me. And for the cover of the CD I selected a truly inspired piece of artwork from the very talented Celine Slator. This was a painting I had bought from Celine some time previously. Imagine my surprise and delight when I discovered that the original title Celine had given to the painting was 'Going Home'!

I feel truly blessed to have been given a meditation from Spirit that has helped many people achieve the right frame of mind to experience the connection that we can have with loved ones no longer in this world. I hope that you too will find it to be of use in your own journey towards Spirit awareness.

7

NOT JUST A MAN TALKING TO HIMSELF – ROB'S STORY

Any one of us has the potential to become a medium. But you may be wondering what kinds of people decide to get involved in this area about which so little is understood. Despite the fact that in all I have said so far I have tried to emphasise the extent to which these things are open and available to everyone, perhaps you are still sceptical. Surely only those with a 'special gift' – or those who have taken leave of their senses! – would choose to go down this path?

By telling you my own story and giving you a flavour of my life before becoming a professional medium, I have tried to highlight the fact that I'm an ordinary guy – someone who makes his way in the world of everyday life, someone with a family who lives a lot of his life very much like everyone else. However, you still may not be convinced. So I want to share with you in this chapter the story of my first 'student', Robert. While his story is remarkable in its own right, you will see that Robert is in many ways a regular guy, who had the same questions and concerns most people have when they first think about looking further into the world of Spirit. In Chapter 11, we will look at the story of another of my regular circle members, Lurleen. The purpose of sharing these stories is to show you that everyone has the ability to develop their mediumistic abilities to connect and communicate with the Spirit World, no matter where they come from, or what their background or life experiences have been.

Robert Wright – Rob – was one of the first people to come along to my circle group and channelling classes. He is someone that I admire for his strengths, his dedication to Spirit and his determination to get things done. Here, in his own words, is Rob's account of his journey so far:

> My spiritual story really began to first take shape during the summer of 2004. My mother had gone for an angel card reading from a lady who came highly recommended. Afterwards, Mam told me about the reading she'd just

received and how the information had been extremely accurate. The thing that intrigued me the most was the information that had come through concerning an uncle of mine who had passed away some years before. Mam said that certain things had been described in great detail, that names had been given of people who had passed, with information about their lives and the times they had spent with her – and all of it was absolutely correct.

I will admit to being sceptical, but something was drawing me to book a reading for myself. So I phoned and spoke to Ann, and proceeded to ask her if she would do an angel card reading for me. I was delighted when she said I'd only be waiting a week, so I agreed a time and I hung up the phone. When Mam asked if I'd made the appointment, I shrugged it off a bit and said, 'Yes, the angel woman's going to tell my fortune', making a joke of it in an attempt to be macho and to hide the fact I was actually looking forward to it.

The day of the reading arrived and I found myself outside Ann's door. When I knocked, this tiny slim woman answered and immediately threw her arms around me and greeted me with, 'Rob, me auld flower!' Let me explain – I'm six foot and of quite a big build, so when I hugged Ann back, she disappeared, only to emerge again with a huge smile. She radiated boundless energy and quickly informed me that she had so much to tell me that she couldn't wait.

I followed Ann into the room where she does her readings and found that I was surrounded by the most beautiful painted images of archangels, all over the walls. The air in the room felt different – lighter – and there was the softest music on in the background. I felt as though I was surrounded by angels – something I later found out to be true.

During that reading, Ann explained that around me were angels and all I had to do was ask for them and they would be there. I laughed and told her that if I admitted to mates that I was 'calling on my angels', they'd make a laughing stock of me. I told her I was a man's man and that this airy-fairy stuff wouldn't help me and then let her get on with the reading. I was given information about a change of career and was told that my new job would involve healing. Ann explained that a piece of paper would make it clear and that things would fall into place and the new job would be mine for the taking.

About two weeks after the reading, I was at work on a damp, cold Friday morning. I was just signing in when I saw a notice on the board advertising a job for a healthcare assistant. I read the notice and it said all applications had to be submitted by four o'clock that evening. I remembered what Ann had told me during the reading, about my next job involving healing. I just smiled to myself and thought, *what a coincidence*. After studying the notice, I realised that

I had no CV to hand and that I wouldn't get time to do one before the deadline, so I went to start work.

As I was walking away from the sign-in desk, my boss appeared and in the course of chatting, she said that the floor was overstaffed that day. Something went off in my head – it was like a flash – and I turned and asked if it was possible to get a holiday and take the day off. My boss smiled and said I'd be doing her a favour if I could take the day off. So I went home, drew up a CV, got together all the appropriate documents and managed to bring everything into the office before the deadline. Two weeks later I had my interview. Two days after that, I was offered the job.

I've now been seven years working on a ward for elderly patients, caring for and helping them in their everyday lives. That whole incident really opened my eyes to what Ann had told me – not only the new career, but the way everything had fallen into place, so that I was able to apply for the job in time. I knew in my heart that this was the work of my angels.

In light of all that had happened, I started going to angel seminars and buying books and cards and so on, just to try to increase my knowledge and understanding of how angels could be working in my life. I kept bumping into Ann at seminars and other events, and each time would be greeted with the big smile and hug and of course the usual, 'Rob, me auld flower!' It was like having a personal hug and welcome from my own angel. I soon realised that anybody Ann was around got this hug and smile, and felt as wonderful as I did just being in this remarkable woman's presence.

It wasn't long before I went back to Ann for another reading. This time I was told about my spiritual path ahead. Ann said that I would soon be standing in front of people doing my work – giving messages from Spirit. Once again I denied it, saying there was 'no way' that anything like this would happen. Ann just looked at me and said, 'Yes, it will. The angels have told me.'

Then, through Ann, I received a message from my cousin Joe, who had passed away tragically a short time earlier. To my astonishment Ann was able to tell me how he passed and she even gave the date he passed. When explaining the message from Joe, she kept saying that he was a very lively guy and a bit of a rogue. She didn't make him out to be saintly, but just told me who he was and described him perfectly, flaws and all. This was a real eye-opener for me, because any medium I'd gone to in the past had always given a picture of people who have passed on as saints – when in actual fact, they were not too saintly in character at all!

When the reading was drawing to a close, Ann kept saying she'd love me to meet her son Tom. She said we had the same energy and would get along great. Again, it proved to be true.

Eighteen months had gone by and, spiritually, not a lot had been going on for me. I still went to Ann for the odd reading but not a lot more than that was happening. Then one day I received a phone call from Ann, asking if I'd be interested in attending an angel class she now had up and running. I jumped at the chance and said I'd be going along that Wednesday and couldn't wait.

When I turned up for the class that Wednesday evening, I felt nervous going in, as I'd no idea what was involved or expected of me. That night however, there was to be a change of plan: instead of Ann leading the class, her son Tom would be taking it, and instead of focusing on angels, we would now be doing mediumship. I had no inclination towards mediumship – to be honest, I didn't really know what a medium did – and so this just added to the nerves that were already there.

I was the first to arrive for the class. Ann and Tom were already there, preparing the room. I introduced myself to Tom and chatted about this and that. Ann told me it was going to be a great night. So I sat down and waited in nervous anticipation of what lay ahead. Other people started to arrive. I soon noticed that, of all the thirty or so people in the class, I was the only male. This made me even more uneasy. I was well and truly out of my comfort zone!

When the class started, Tom began by saying, 'It's great to have a male energy in the circle this evening.' At this, all the women looked in my direction and I just kept thinking, *Oh my God, I'm mortified!*

The class started with a meditation and after that people in the circle gave information about spirits who had come through with messages. I sat back in amazement. There were women giving the most astounding messages for people and even more amazingly, the people who received the messages didn't know those who were giving them at all.

During all of this, Tom was at the top of class, linking in and helping relay parts of the various messages, while Ann was holding the energy in the room [supporting the energy of the people in circle and the energy of Spirit to allow the energies to blend together so a communication can happen]. It was fantastic. At the end of the evening, I thanked Tom and Ann, and went home wondering how people could do such a thing – give messages and be so accurate. I decided to buy some books, to try to get as much information as I could on mediumship before the next class.

Because the circle was the last Wednesday of every month, I had a lot of time to digest what had gone on in that first class. I was keen to go again but only to observe, I decided, as I thought I didn't have the talent or know-how to give messages. The next class started just as the first had, but during the meditation, I had visions of my grandfather who had long since passed. He was talking to me about my mam and dad and about other family members. It was great to have this vision, and I felt really happy and contented. When my granddad had said all he wanted to say, we said our goodbyes, and I opened my eyes and came out of my meditation. I noticed that I was the only one who was no longer meditating, and I sat quietly, so as not to disturb the class.

As I sat there, I closed my eyes for a few moments. All at once I got an image of two young lads walking with a big white horse. They had very broad Dublin accents and were shouting at each other. I could see this scene as clear as day and could hear every word of their conversation.

While I was watching all of this, I'd failed to realise that everyone else in the class had come out of the meditation. I opened my eyes to find them all looking at me intently. I thought to myself, I'm not saying what I saw – people will think I'm mad! So I just sat there and said nothing. Then I looked up to where Tom was sitting and he looked at me and said, 'Rob, tell the two lads the horse will be fine – and ask them what they have to say.'

Without thinking, I roared up at Tom, 'You can see that?'

He laughed and just said yes.

In disbelief I asked, 'What have I to do?'

'Just ask them what they'd like to say,' Tom replied.

So I asked and they answered, saying that they were looking to talk to their ma. They said her name was Mags and that they missed her. Thankfully the lady sitting across from me understood the information – she had been hoping her boys would come through and give her some message, to let her know they were all right. It was a brief exchange, but all that their mother needed. I remember just sitting there after that, thinking how good a feeling it was to be able to help someone in this way. And to this day, whenever I give a message, the feeling is the same as the first time I ever connected with those in the Spirit World.

After that, I attended every circle meeting and soon became friends with Tom. Under his tuition, my ability to connect with Spirit increased all the time, with many connections being made and many messages being both given and received. That circle continued for many years, and I met many fantastic healers, mediums and friends along the way.

Some time after I started attending this circle, another one was started, this time in Celbridge, which Tom invited me to join. This group was going to be smaller and more structured, as it was to eventually become a 'closed circle'. This meant that once the right number of members had joined and the right energy was established, the circle would be restricted to those people from then on. I jumped at this chance to develop my mediumship further and began attending both circles. Each group had a different dynamic but both were fantastic in terms of the people who came along and the messages that came through and were passed on. Soon the Celbridge circle was going so well that very quickly, by popular demand, it became a fortnightly group rather than a monthly one, and then it went from every two weeks to every week.

It was through the Celbridge circle that the information about the Arthur Findlay College in Stansted came to light. Tom had been over there and had come back, talking excitedly about this fabulous place and the courses that they were running. A group of seven of us from the Celbridge Circle decided to book a course and we wasted no time in paying our deposits and arranging our travel.

Arriving in Stansted on 4 April 2009, I was eagerly anticipating a new phase in my spiritual progression. Two circle friends, Dolores and James, accompanied me. The other four of our party were to arrive on a later flight, so the three of us got a taxi to the college based in a magnificent stately home set in acres of beautiful landscaped garden – but as we approached it via a long driveway lined with tall trees on that misty April morning, it was truly an exceptional sight.

When the others from our group arrived, we all went to meet the tutor of the course. After a brief interview, he put us into groups. There were 160 people on the course, divided into six groups. The group I was in also had two people from the circle at home in Celbridge: a lady called Ann and my dear, sweet friend, Dolores.

Our tutor was a fantastic lady by the name of Julie Gris: a very direct-speaking woman and an extremely knowledgeable medium. During the course of that week, Julie showed me how to connect with Spirit in a more direct way, as well as passing on many techniques and tips that would help prepare me to use my mediumship abilities professionally.

As the course unfolded, I saw and learned about many forms of spiritual work, from Tai Chi, to 'trance' mediumship, to 'direct voice' mediumship. I also got to partake in various things I previously had no opportunity to. I was sharing a room with Tom and James, so at the end of each day I could discuss the different things with Tom and learn about what his group was doing too.

Throughout the week, people were chosen from each group to do a demonstration of mediumship in front of an audience at the end of each day. Friday was the last day for demonstrations and I was asked if I would demonstrate that afternoon. I reluctantly agreed: I was very nervous at the idea.

I had told everyone who had come with me from the Celbridge circle, and they said they'd go to support me when it was my turn to take the stage. But it turned out that Tom had booked a private reading that day at 2 o'clock – the time the demonstrations were starting. So he asked me to see if I could go last – that way he could make it down to see me. But I was afraid of messing up my reading, so I asked to go first, thinking that if things did go wrong for me, at least Tom wouldn't be there to see it. However, I was told that I had been allocated the last spot and that the time couldn't be changed. I felt physically weak.

When the demonstration started, they asked the back three rows of the audience to move to another venue where another demo was being held, as there weren't enough people there. A few from our Celbridge group got up, but then I saw Dolores say that she was staying to support me – and it made my heavy heart light. There I was, nervous, feeling sick – but this gesture made me see that all I could do was my best, and that no matter what, I'd have all the support in the world. It felt like Dolores was an angel sent to help me: my angel Dolores. Knowing she and my Spirit guides were there for me, I was able to get through my platform demo unscathed, and even managed to bring through some good information for some of my audience …

After we had returned home from that incredible week at the Arthur Findlay College, we all continued to attend the circles, but something felt different. We were on a high and incorporated everything we had learned on the course into our work within the circle. As well as the feeling that we had each made huge leaps forward in developing our mediumship and work with Spirit, something else very positive came out of our time in Stansted: the founding of the first Spiritualist church in Ireland. The idea had arisen out of a series of discussions between the seven of us who had attended the course. We all agreed that it was so much easier for the mediums from Britain who, after the week's training was over, could go back to various Spiritualist churches and perform their mediumship on platforms for audiences who had come along specifically for that purpose. We knew that if we could set up a Spiritualist church in Ireland, people would at last have a place to go and witness mediumship on a regular basis, and attend circles for all forms of spiritual work.

I was honoured to be given a role on the committee of the newly founded Spiritualist Union of Ireland (SUI), with a responsibility for events. I initially was nervous about this new-found pressure, as I had never done anything like this before. But I was excited and I knew that I was working for Spirit and that I should put my trust in its guidance.

The opening night of the SUI was a truly great occasion for me. I had arranged the medium's speaker's chair and music, and had decided that the mediums who had worked so hard to get the place up and running should be those to demonstrate that night. So, with my fellow committee members, I had the opportunity to demonstrate my mediumship from a platform for the first time in Ireland. I was really humbled to get the chance to do a platform with Tom, who had been my teacher from the beginning.

The demonstration went brilliantly that night and the room was full to capacity. It seemed we had reached out to people who were looking for a spiritual centre and that all our work was worth it.

Since then my work as a medium has gone from strength to strength. Although I had been doing private, one-to-one sittings before, the demand for readings was growing all the time. Soon my schedule was completely full – between my mediumship work and my role helping to run our spiritual centre. My life had turned around completely and my work with Spirit was now the main focus for my time, exactly as Ann had predicted right at the start.

All of this is very fulfilling and I couldn't be happier. As well as for my wonderful parents, Jude and Catherine, and my friends and colleagues, I am forever grateful for my guiding light and soul mate, Dolores Malone, now Mrs Wright after we got married in a Spiritual Wedding Ceremony on 25 October 2013, who helped me up when I fell and who now holds my heart with such care and affection, and for Tracy, another angel on earth, for always telling me exactly how it is, good, bad or indifferent.

Most of all, I am grateful every single day to Spirit, without whose guidance and help I'm just a man talking to himself.

Robert Wright

8

INVESTIGATING SPIRIT

In my role as a working medium, I have been involved in a number of investigations of Spirit activity – or paranormal investigations – in castles, houses and other venues around Ireland. I greatly enjoy this type of work: going to different places all over the country, connecting with the energy of a building and establishing contact with the Spirit people associated with that venue.

It is another fascinating aspect of mediumship: a paranormal investigation team will bring instruments such as thermometers, infra-red cameras, sound-recording equipment, motion detectors etc. that can indicate the presence of a spirit. These can shed more light on the world of Spirit and bring further evidence through. While my own approach is largely a spiritual one, based on my own religious beliefs, I also respect the scientific standpoint and believe it should also be taken into account. There is no reason why the two approaches shouldn't complement one another.

Although the signs of Spirit activity in a building may be unnerving and even upsetting, especially for those who live there, I am always keen to point out to people that these are just ways of Spirit making its presence felt, and that Spirit people are there to connect and communicate with us – not to harm or to frighten us. House owners will tell of knocking and banging noises, or the sound of footsteps; of seeing shadows or sensing presences; of feeling something brush off them or bedclothes being tugged; TV channels being changed and lights going on and off without explanation. None of these phenomena are anything to be afraid of – these are just instances of Spirit trying to make contact with us.

Sometimes a spirit may stay earthbound if it feels it has something to complete, or should for some reason stay around the family for a while – as in the film *Ghost*, for example, where the character played by Patrick Swayze stays around his partner to try to protect her from harm. Earthbound spirits are depicted well in *Ghost Whisperer*, the TV show that has James van Praagh, the well-known psychic medium, as one of its executive producers.

A question I am often asked is whether I believe in malevolent Spirit. My answer is always that I don't believe in negative Spirit, but that I have encountered *troubled* Spirit individuals. In my view, troubled spirits are generally earthbound spirits who may not actually realise they have passed – and if they were troubled or unhappy while living in the physical world, then they will bring through the same energy in their earthbound state. Not being aware that they have passed, such spirits may continue to do the same day-to-day things as in their previous lives – so if they were a negative person while on the physical plane they will continue to project in the same way. Some people may perceive this as being malevolent, but in my view this is not at all the case.

~

In March 2010 I got a call from reporter Kevin Jenkinson from the *Irish Daily Star*, asking if I would be prepared to help investigate some paranormal activity in a house in Finglas. The owners of the house had also contacted *The Gerry Ryan Show* to talk about the troubling happenings they were experiencing regularly in their home. So some of the broadcasting team from Gerry's show would be there to record the investigation, as well as Mark Guerin from PIGS (the Paranormal Investigation Guys), a paranormal investigation outfit based in Dublin.

John and Helen Emmett and their family, who had been living in the house for some years, were feeling stressed and exhausted by the Spirit activity in the house, as Kevin Jenkinson's follow-up article in the *Star* at the time highlighted:

> 'I've had it with this fella, he seems to be attacking the men in the family, but we are not leaving,' said former soldier John Emmett, who has seen a tall dark figure hover past him …

John and his wife Helen described how every month the paranormal activity would escalate, creating a feeling of anger and hate in the house, making them argue and feel claustrophobic. 'It's hard to describe how strong this bad feeling would be. If it had its way, we would be out of here,' said John.

'I used to wake up at night, wondering where my sheet had gone and would find it laid out perfectly under the bed, and as I put it back over me, something would pull at it,' said Nathan Emmett [their son], who has since moved out of the house.

John's wife Helen said their young grandchildren have spoken of a 'shadow man' standing in the corner of the small box room at the back of the house, looking at them as they slept – and one saw a tall, dark figure pass through the window. Electronic devices, such as radios and the kettle, would switch on by themselves. The family have heard footsteps on their stairway; items have slammed to the ground or moved without anyone touching them, and things have gone missing.

Gary Emmett, another son who has also moved out of the house, recorded eerie whispers over fifteen years ago, and took a photograph in a bedroom of a blue orb that appears to have a face inside it.

'Whenever it gets really bad, and I know it's in the room, I just sing anything that comes into my head and tell it to leave, and it does,' said Helen.

When I arrived at the house in Finglas on the day of the investigation, I met with everyone gathered there: the Emmetts, Kevin from the *Star*, Mark Guerin and his colleagues from PIGS and some of the team from RTÉ 2FM. As I chatted with John and Helen, they began to tell me more about what they were experiencing, and I was quickly aware that there was a very heavy, oppressive-feeling energy to the place.

The paranormal team busied themselves setting up some of the various pieces of equipment they had brought with them to take temperature readings and record sound. Even as we sat in the living room, the PIGS guys were able to tell us that, within the space of fifteen minutes, there had been a sudden drop in temperature, with the thermometer reader falling from thirty-two degrees Celsius to twenty-one degrees. All of my experiences have confirmed that Spirit energy often comes through as a cold feeling and sensation.

I went upstairs for an initial recce, accompanied by Kevin the reporter, a photographer and a member of the investigation team. In all three of the upstairs rooms, I was immediately aware of three separate Spirit presences. In the third room, the box room, I sensed an earthbound spirit energy – a very heavy, cold energy with an aggressive demeanour. 'There is a very vocal energy in here,' I told the others. 'A tall, strong countryman – about six foot three, with large hands – who died of a sudden heart attack. He is extremely bitter and angry.' He was determined to talk.

I gave the information that was coming through this presence, as well as the two other Spirit contacts, while Kevin took detailed notes.

Then Kevin and I went back downstairs, while the

investigation team did what they needed to do, taking readings with their equipment and so on. Mark from PIGS was saying he could feel a presence in the kitchen, so I followed him in there, accompanied by some of the investigation team, and Kevin, Helen and her husband John.

Straight away, I was drawn to a particular corner. I began to give detailed information to the Emmetts. This fourth spirit was a relative of John's and came through with dates, names, personality traits, conditions of passing and so on, all of which the family were able to verify. The spirit in the kitchen and two of those upstairs had already passed over to the Spirit World, and so there was no sense of troubled energy around them. All appeared to have been linked to the Emmett family: a man who took part in the 1916 Rising, a child who died through miscarriage and a brother of John's who had loved hunting.

Once I had finished communicating with the Spirit loved one in the kitchen, I went back upstairs to the cold box room, along with Kevin the reporter, Helen and her son. The dark, heavy energy was still very much present and I began to attune in order to make some kind of connection. Kevin's article for the *Star* sums up well what happened next:

> Tom said the family of this man used to own the land the house is on when it was a farm in the early part of the 20th century, and [that the spirit] is bitter over his brothers getting a bigger share of the land in their inheritance. Tom believes the man is an 'earthbound spirit' that has not crossed over and can't see the light that is thought to be the gateway which opens when spirits end their physical experience in a human body.
>
> 'He may not realise or know he is dead; he feels threatened by people living on his land and is trying to confront them,' said the medium.
>
> Tom proceeded to calm the spirit before directing it towards a bright, white light where he sensed two women, possibly the Spirit's mother and sister, coming to welcome him into the other world.

I had used a scene rescue to bring the spirit back to a place in the past where it was calm, quiet and relaxed, and then loved ones came from the light to help him cross over. Later Kevin and Helen were able to tell me that as soon as the spirit had stepped over into the light and the portal had closed, they could feel the room getting warmer and lighter in energy. And this feeling of calm and peace was, thankfully, to persist after our visit, as Helen later told the *Star*: 'The place was grand and quiet that night. It was the nicest feeling I have ever had in the house, and we really hope it stays like that.'

Strangely enough, *The Gerry Ryan Show* team found that they were unable to broadcast live from the house during the investigation, due to the fact that their sound equipment was playing up. Therefore, in the days that followed, Gerry was keen to do on air some kind of follow-up report on the investigation. I was asked to give an update on what had happened since, while Helen Emmett was also on hand to talk about her experiences.

For those of you who do not know of Gerry Ryan, at that time he was one of Ireland's best-loved broadcasters. If anyone had a problem of any kind, they could ring Gerry and he would try to help them solve it if he could. Gerry was not one for paranormal 'mumbo-jumbo hocus-pocus', as he had referred to it on a number of previous occasions. So I was prepared for plenty of wisecracks and a lot of scepticism from Gerry when they rang me for the interview. Anyway, I began by describing the spirits that we connected with in the Emmetts' house, dwelling particularly on Arthur (which, as we had learned in the interim, was the troubled spirit's name). I talked about the five 'clair' senses, and said that we can all connect and communicate with those in the Spirit World.

Gerry's next question was to Helen: he wanted to know how they were going to deal with the problem in the house in the future. He was clearly completely taken aback when she said that the energy in the house had very much changed since we had helped Arthur, the earthbound spirit, cross over into the light. Helen confirmed that the feeling of anger in the box room was gone, as was the impression of those in the house being watched all the time: these had been replaced by an energy that was light and warm. Gerry asked me to describe how this had been achieved and listened intently when I explained that in my opinion, earthbound spirits will not harm you, and that any disturbances they cause to happen, such as banging and knocking and so on, are harmless and just a sign of a spirit's frustration when people appear to be ignoring it and not engaging with its efforts to communicate. As I commented to a number of people after the interview, Gerry was definitely different in his approach to the Spirit World on that occasion, compared to the past. He was far more accepting and less critical – there was not one smart or derogatory comment from him. (The full interview with Gerry is on my website, www.tomcolton.com, under the 'News' section.)

Gerry Ryan himself returned to the Spirit World on

30 April 2010, some five weeks after I did that radio interview with him. He was found dead in his apartment: it would later emerge that he had suffered a heart attack. The minute I heard the news of his death, I felt a pain in my chest and I told Ann, my mother, to whom I was talking on the phone at that time, that I felt Gerry had passed from a heart attack: something which was later confirmed.

Perhaps the reason that Gerry had been so different in his approach, showing understanding and acceptance of the Spirit World when he had done that last interview with Helen and me, was that he knew in his heart and soul that he, too, was soon to return to Spirit himself. I know that his mother, to whom he was very close, passed to the Spirit World in 2006, and this took a lot out of him. Perhaps he knew that he was soon to be reunited with her.

I remember that one of the many newspaper articles published after Gerry Ryan's death made reference to the fact that he had always said he knew he was not going to live beyond a certain age. You often hear stories of people saying they don't have much time left before passing over to the Spirit World. I think that deep down we do know when we will return to Spirit, because we have already chosen our path before coming here by choosing our story and putting it together like the script of a film. It is my firm belief that, before we come to this earth, we decide who our parents are going to be, when we are going to be born, the circumstances of our lives, how we will pass and when we pass – and everything in between.

~

I first met Sam Stone, who is the founder of a small, non-profit paranormal investigation group in County Kildare called Soul Searchers, when he kindly invited me to participate in a Halloween fund-raising event he was putting together. Since Soul Searchers have been in operation, they have invited many mediums and psychics to participate in their investigations. Compared to those of other paranormal investigating groups, their approach is quite diverse and inclusive, as they are not only interested in the scientific evidence, but like to take into account the less tangible, spiritual evidence also.

At the Halloween event I gave a demonstration of mediumship, and afterwards Sam said that I had impressed both him and many of the audience members with the type of information I was able to bring through. Not long after that Sam invited me to take part in one of his team's first pub investigations. The pub in question was situated in County Kildare. The owner had given Sam an insight into the history of the building and business, and, as always, Sam had taken notes, which he could later compare to the information that I would bring forward through my connection with the Spirit World. This is Sam's fascinating first-hand account of the investigation:

> We all arrived together [at the pub], at 11.30 p.m. on 29 November 2010. To say that it was a cold night would be an understatement! Before we entered the pub, Tom stopped me outside and pointed towards the top floor. When I asked why he was pointing to the upstairs level, he whispered. 'He's up there ... Fire ... fire – he died there!' As Tom followed the rest of the team into the pub, I was left outside, thinking and still looking up. I knew then that this was going to be an interesting evening.
>
> The pub was located on the ground floor; office space took up the upper three floors. After Tom had adjusted to the surroundings, he decided that he needed to go upstairs, where he was initially sensing the spirit of the young man who had passed over. Before we left the downstairs pub area, I asked him did he feel anything in the actual pub itself. He explained that the [original] surroundings had not been much different to how it looked now, and went

on to further describe the layout as was, saying that during recent years an extension had been added. I took notes as he shared the information, but I already knew that he had described it perfectly, as the owner had described it all to me earlier.

To get to the upper floors we had to enter a hall from a side door that was located outside the premises. This led to a set of stairs, taking us to the first floor, which was occupied by office rooms. I asked Tom if he would like to enter these rooms to see what he might sense. But he insisted that we should all go to the third floor – the top floor.

As we began to get closer to the area where Tom was sensing the spirit of a young man, I noticed him becoming much more breathless. I asked if he would like to take a break. But he insisted that we keep going, until we came to a stop outside the very top room.

The team focused on Tom and I, as I stood right beside him. He began explaining, giving us more information about this spirit. The more he explained, the more I noticed his breathing becoming erratic. It was almost as if he was reliving this young man's horrific death. The spirit, he claimed, had moved on, but this tragic memory was still very much lingering in the atmosphere. I always tend to stay neutral when working with mediums, yet at this particular moment, I couldn't help but feel quite hesitant, due to the fact that the temperature was rising and, very oddly, I was being met now by a smell of smoke.

Our temperature devices confirmed a dramatic change in temperature in the place Tom had led us to. Tom felt that the young man had tried to escape from the building, but had become trapped and died in this room. The constant change in Tom's breathing was mirroring the breathlessness the young man must have experienced as he inhaled the fatal smoke fumes.

After this, Tom visited some of the other rooms, claiming that the building had once been a hotel. But, strangely, he refused to enter one particular room: it was almost as if he physically couldn't. When I asked him why, he explained that the 'energy' in the room was too much to bear. At the time I couldn't understand his resistance to entering the room, but later it would all make sense.

These were the main highlights regarding Tom's information, information that already to me rang true and matched my notes very well. But I usually like to go through all the details scrupulously over the next day or so after an investigation, and when I did this, I was extremely impressed.

Several days after the investigation, the local historical society contacted me to say that they had been able to source records from the early part of the twentieth century, which confirmed what Tom had told us to be true. It seemed that in the 1930s, a young man had indeed died in the very room Tom had led us to. There had been a fire in the building, and this young guy had become trapped while trying to escape and had died of smoke inhalation. It also seemed that the premises had been used as a hotel for many years, from the early 1800s to the mid-1980s!

How could Tom have possibly known all of this, especially when this information could only be verified later from records that weren't on public display anywhere? The information that he was able to access through his mediumship had really impressed us all, as well as many other people, including the local paper, the *Leinster Leader*, who were very interested in doing a story.

An 'energy' footprint is left behind wherever people have been, very much like a fingerprint we would leave on the handle of a door when we open it or on a window if we place our hand on the glass. The 'tragic memory' mentioned in Sam's account is an example of this. The room I didn't want to enter was currently being used for energy work and a lot of people's 'stuff' (negative energy) was in the room. When we are doing investigation work at places to find out what may have happened there, as mediums we look for these energy footprints as well as trying to communicate with any spirits that are there.

~

I got a call from Niall Boylan (radio presenter and DJ) in early October 2009. Niall was in the process of setting up Real Radio and had just been granted a one-month licence to broadcast as a tester station. During the month in question I got the opportunity to contribute to a few of the new station's programmes. On one occasion I was asked to do a live telephone interview about why Halloween is significant in the context of connecting with the Spirit World. After about twenty minutes chatting with the presenters, they asked me out of the blue if I would try connecting with someone in the Spirit World there and then – live on air. They were not ready for what was about to happen …

Trying to tune out the pressure of knowing that I was on live radio, I focused hard on attuning to the Spirit World. Almost immediately, I was able to connect with a Spirit lady, who began to channel some very specific information through me. I told one of the presenters that I was connected with someone associated with him, and started to pass on these details I was being given. The information flowed and flowed. After a silence at the other end of the line, one of the presenters started crying and said, 'That's my grandmother to a tee!' The other presenter then explained to the listeners what had happened, noting with amazement how accurately I had connected with her colleague's grandmother – so much so that he had been brought to tears, live on radio. It was incredibly moving to have made that connection possible and that the information had come through so accurately and seamlessly. (Again, you can find a recording of the full radio interview on the 'News' page of my website: www.tomcolton.com.)

From this time, Niall Boylan (who is currently working on 4FM) and I stayed in regular contact, even though he is a big sceptic. Not long afterwards, I suggested to him that we set up a Spirit investigation for Halloween, in which we could invite some of his show's listeners to participate. So the production team contacted Mark Guerin from PIGS, who, as I have mentioned, I also worked with for *The Gerry Ryan Show*. Mark suggested that we investigate the basement of the National Leprechaun Museum in Dublin, which is a museum dedicated to Irish folklore.

While this basement had previously been used as a venue for the Dublin Paranormal Convention, no one had ever investigated it to see what was actually down there. It was well known that the basement had housed a mortuary back in the 1800s, when the building across the road from it (now a shopping centre) had been the

Jervis Street Hospital. The outer walls of the basement also sat on a boundary of St Mary's graveyard, meaning that in some places, bodies in the graveyard were buried only four feet away.

Mark and I were invited onto the 4FM *Late Show* to do a pre-event promotion. We started off by talking about the investigation and what it would entail, explaining that we were hoping to bring some of the listeners along with us to witness the event live on air. We then asked listeners to ring in to share their ghostly ghoul stories, which some of them did. I also did a few live readings for other listeners. Meanwhile, over the course of the evening, a number of people were selected to join us on our mission to investigate the basement of the Leprechaun Museum.

It wasn't long before the 'Fright Night Special', as it had been dubbed, was upon us. The sense of excitement in the run-up to the event – on radio shows, Facebook and in the media – was truly electric. Everyone was wishing all the participating listeners and the presenters luck; some were even saying that they were afraid for the listeners.

Sometime before we were due to go live, we all met up at the museum to prepare for the broadcast and do the various sound checks and so on. The team included presenters Niall Boylan, Niall O'Keeffe and Suzanne

Kane, all of whom had radio mikes to record any sounds and happenings over the next few hours; there was also a video crew with night-vision equipment, so that the night's events could be filmed in their entirety.

Once we were all ready to go, we entered the basement, going down the steps to the area where the dead bodies would have been brought into the morgue from the hospital across the road. I was one of the last to make the descent. As I did, I could feel the presence of Spirit starting to connect with me. When I got to the bottom of the flight of steps, I started to shiver uncontrollably. I could feel the presence of a man who had passed from pneumonia and whose whole body shook as he lay dying from the condition. I was able to describe this gentleman physically, and I also got the details of his name and the precise condition from which he had passed.

Next, we all went into another, larger room, directly under the museum building. We gathered to wait together and see what we could pick up and whether any spirits would connect with us. The room was quite active. As we started to link up with the energies around us, I quickly found myself being drawn to the back wall, where I started coughing. I could feel the sensation of smoke in my lungs and was finding it very hard to breathe. It soon became clear that I was connecting with a gentleman who had died from smoke inhalation during a fire. I felt that his remains had been buried in the graveyard behind the place in the wall that I had been drawn to.

We started to do a few 'callings out', which is where you ask spirits to make themselves known to you through any means possible, be it by sound, touch or by moving an object. We started to hear a lot of different sounds and a number of people felt like they were being touched or brushed against. Quite alarmingly, for her, one of the listeners started to feel as if she was being strangled, so I sat her down on a chair and explained to her that this was only a spirit trying to connect, by communicating to her the way in which it had passed to the Spirit World. I assured her that she was not going to be harmed in any way. I then asked the spirit to stand aside and to disconnect from the lady. After a couple of minutes the spirit distanced itself as requested and the listener began to feel noticeably better as the sensation of tightness around her neck started to dissipate.

Not long after this, some of those in our party reported the sensation of being struck by stones being hurled at them. Unexplained noises became more and more frequent, and soon they began to sound more and more like human voices uttering various words. Several people reported hearing the sound of a baby at different times.

At this point, we decided to split the party into two groups. One group would stay in that room, while the rest would go back around to the front of the building, where we had entered. I made my way with the latter group around to the front of the building, and as we did so, we started to connect with a young girl in the corridor. All at once, Suzanne, one of the presenters, screamed and fell to the floor, as she felt the shock of a spirit energy entering her body. 'Oh my God, what was that, what was that?' she kept saying. Here again, trying to keep her calm, I pointed out that the spirits were only trying to connect and communicate with us – that they were not there to do any harm or cause any hurt to anyone. I explained that, very possibly, those earthbound spirits who were occupying this space weren't used to having so many visitors all at once and that it must have felt as if we were invading their territory!

It was then decided that we would try to use the Ouija board as a means of communicating. Mark had with him a board from the 1950s, and the listeners accompanying us tried this traditional tool of communication as a means of bringing through messages from the Spirit World.

Many people frown upon the Ouija board and say that it is dangerous. In my view, however, it is not the board itself that is dangerous: it is those who use it incorrectly who are usually the problem!

Mark placed the Ouija board on a table in one of the smallest rooms in the basement, an area that earlier in the evening had been identified as the holding area for bodies when they were first brought into the mortuary. As we began to communicate using the board, one of the group asked questions and in reply the little mouse-like pointer started moving to indicate a yes or no, and spelled out various facts and details.

We also decided to use a pendulum as a means of connecting and getting information. A pendulum consists of a precious stone on a chain or cord, which moves in different directions as questions are asked of it. One of the individuals in our group started to ask questions relating to her brother who had passed to the Spirit World. She received one answer after another to each question. It was clearly a very emotional experience for the lady in question.

This investigation turned out to be one of the most enjoyable I have ever done. It really felt like everyone in the group experienced a connection of some kind; some of our number were lucky enough to receive some very real and meaningful information from the Spirit World.

I very much enjoy collaborating with those who favour a scientific approach to the manifestations of the Spirit World: it is always rewarding to witness the ways in which their approach and my own, more spiritual take on these matters can coincide and overlap to allow all of us to learn more about the realm of Spirit and its workings.

9

'ARE YOU THERE, SIDNEY?' – THE PROBLEM OF DOUBT

We are spirits clad in veils.

Christopher Pearse Cranch

The title for this chapter is a line from a famous ad for *Toffee Crisp* chocolate bars from many years ago. The ad features a scene where a group of people are sitting at a table in a circle, having a séance. At a certain point, the medium asks, 'Are you there, Sidney?' and as if in reply, the lampshade above them starts to shake and, lo and behold, an empty *Toffee Crisp* wrapper drops onto the table. This is supposedly 'Sidney's' sign from the Spirit World that he is indeed present in the room – since *Toffee Crisp* was his favourite chocolate bar while he was alive.

The ad was a popular one at the time, and indeed very

funny and clever, but in some senses it also had a valid point as far as mediumship goes. As I have said previously, the type of mediumship that I practise – evidential mediumship – is all about connecting to the Spirit World to bring proof of the survival of the spirit after the physical body passes. It is the quality and validity of the evidence that makes for a good communication, and the fact that the sitter or sitters can verify it in a practical way.

One of the biggest challenges for a working medium is when those for whom a Spirit communication is intended do not appear to be able to understand it, or are convinced that it has no relevance for them. When a sitter rejects or cannot acknowledge information I pass on to them from Spirit, there can be a number of explanations. The most common reason tends to be one of the following: the person does not have the factual knowledge of a situation to be able to verify it or otherwise; someone may be so overwhelmed by the feeling of being connected with a Spirit loved one that they may be unable to remember specific details or even experience a complete mental block; or lastly, someone is simply unable or unwilling to let go of their own scepticism, for whatever reason.

The last scenario is the most difficult for a medium, and it can be very frustrating when it seems that a sitter is determined to reject whatever evidence is brought through, no matter how detailed or compelling it may be. I have to say, however, that in my experience there are very few people who will reject convincing evidence just for the sake of it, to be awkward and uncooperative. I believe that this is because very few of us tend to remain unmoved and unaffected when a true connection with Spirit happens.

The most common reason a communication does not resonate with a sitter is that they do not have the knowledge to be able to validate the information or otherwise. This is why I will always ask someone to check with the rest of the family circle or some other external source before rejecting a message out-of-hand. A good example of such a scenario happened with a reading I gave to one of my Celbridge circle members some time ago, a man who very much wanted to make a connection with his father who had recently passed away. Not long into the reading, his dad came through very clearly to me. The father kept indicating the date of one of my sisters' birthdays to me – 14 November, which is when my sister Anita was born. I wasn't entirely sure of the significance of this date for him (this is another example of the indirect way in which Spirit can communicate sometimes), but when I passed this on to his son, my sitter, he confirmed that this was the date his father had passed.

Next the father went on to tell me that he had one of his children in the Spirit World with him – a child who had passed just after being born.

'No,' the sitter said at this. He was adamant. 'There are only the three of us.'

'Your dad is acknowledging four children,' I replied, 'one of whom is in the Spirit World with him.'

'No, definitely not,' he insisted, seeming almost a little upset now. 'I surely would have known if there was another child.'

I asked him gently, however, if he would go and verify the information within the next few days, saying that I could only give him what I was getting from his dad.

The following week, at our next circle meeting, this man told me that after the reading the week before he had asked his mother if he had had another sibling who had been lost to the Spirit World. She confirmed that yes, he had indeed had a brother who died at birth. She explained that she and his father had never spoken of this child, or told their children about him, as it was difficult to talk about and would have been very painful to explain at the time.

Another memorable instance, when verification came only some time after the event, happened during my first ever public demonstration in 2008. At one point in the evening I established a very strong connection with a child's energy from the Spirit World. All at once this little boy was standing beside me, holding in his hand what I can only describe as a teddy bear exactly like the one Mr Bean has, all flopped over on itself. I gave the audience the information the child was giving me as evidence – about the circumstances of his passing, his father's name and some other details. I then asked, 'Does anyone understand this little boy in the Spirit World?' There was silence.

Then one gentleman put up his hand and said, 'I understand some of it, but not all of it.'

'No, sorry,' I said, 'I'm not connected with you.' As a medium you will feel clearly when a connection is right – and, even though this man had come forward, I didn't feel that I had yet connected with the boy's relative, but I knew he or she was somewhere in the audience.

Although no one else signalled that they could take the information, I decided to proceed regardless. 'I am going to give more of the information anyway,' I explained. 'I know there is a connection somewhere here for this little boy, so I will share with you what he is telling me.'

So I continued giving the information. After a couple of minutes a lady put up her hand and said, 'Tom, I can take that – I understand everything you are referring to.' She had hesitated in fact because she had just got a reading from me and was afraid to take a second reading.

Now the little boy was showing me his body laid out in a coffin, with his little teddy bear beside him. He brought my attention to a tear in the right arm of the teddy, up where the arm was attached to the shoulder. The sitter who had come forward was not sure about the tear in the toy's arm, she said, but she could completely relate to the description of the teddy bear and confirm that it had been placed in the coffin with the child – who, she said she now knew, was her nephew, the child of her brother. So I asked her if she could check this detail with her brother when she next saw him. The little Spirit boy stayed with me for a while longer after the exchange that evening – he was very persistent and wanted me to make sure the information was verified so that his loved ones would realise that he was indeed there; he also wanted me to assure them that he was okay.

The next day I got a phone call from the lady in question. She excitedly told me that she had been able to speak to her brother and that he had confirmed that when they had placed the teddy bear in the coffin beside his son, they had noticed a tear in the right arm of the toy, where the arm was attached to the shoulder. Such validations of the information I bring through always delight me, for they are confirmation of the existence of the Spirit World and of the fact that our loved ones never really leave us. As a working medium, I am always very grateful to receive this kind of feedback, as it also helps me to build up my encyclopaedia of signs and symbols that the Spirit World may give me to explain certain circumstances and situations.

Another reason that a sitter might not be able to understand in the moment how certain information relates to them is that sometimes people can get what we call 'psychic amnesia' in a reading situation. It can be a very emotional and intense experience and in the tension of the moment, they may not remember information relating to their loved ones and family – particularly when it comes to obscure details. Sometimes people will only make the necessary connections in their mind after the event, when they are more relaxed.

It can also be that a sitter is trying to concentrate so hard on the information from the Spirit World, that they sometimes cannot place the details. As a medium,

I always strive to bring through information that only those very close to the Spirit loved one will be aware of – and so it stands to reason that sometimes people need to check certain things with family and friends afterwards. Time and again, the testimonials people send me about the work I have done with them tell of how a reading made sense to them once they'd had time to reflect.

Unfortunately, however, sometimes there is absolutely no pleasing some people. No matter how much evidence you give them – no matter how much obscure information about a Spirit loved one's memories, personality traits and practical circumstances that only the family would understand – some people can never be satisfied and will always want more and more, or something different. To doubt is human of course, and my whole focus as an evidential medium is to address the perfectly normal scepticism so many of us have at first. But sadly there are some cases where all of my efforts to bring through the most convincing evidence are simply wasted.

I always remember one particularly difficult encounter I had during an evening demonstration of mediumship, which was part of my 'Feel the Spirit' tour in 2009. I always try to be very accepting of the different ways in which people respond to having a reading done – but on this occasion, I found it very difficult to understand the attitude of those concerned.

As with all my demonstrations, at this event, I was doing a mix of photo and general readings. At one point in the evening, an older lady suddenly came through to me: she was singing a particular song. (I can't remember the name of the song now, but do remember that it was an unusual one.) Anyway, I connected the communication with a lady in the audience and explained that I had her mother with me. I started to pass on details about the circumstances of the Spirit loved one's death, and was also able to bring through a description of her very funny and jolly personality. The audience got a good laugh from the information that was coming through about this lady, who had obviously been a live wire and a bit of a character! All of this was acknowledged by the sitter, who seemed very moved and excited that such a connection to her mother had been made.

At this point, I asked whether the sitter would like to come up onto the stage to experience her mother's energy. She had come to the event with her sisters, and now they began to have a debate about who should go up to the front. At last they decided that the lady who had been talking on the microphone – the one I had been addressing as the sitter – should go up to connect with their mother. So up she came and I went through the usual procedure: asking her for permission to allow the Spirit loved one to enter her body and gently guiding her as the sitter, and her mother as the Spirit person, through the process. Soon the lady said she could feel her mother's energy really strongly, and she started to cry as the experience was so intense. I then asked her mother to separate her energy and stand aside, which she did. The lady went back to her seat in the audience.

Pleased to have been able to make such a successful connection for this lady and her sisters, I started to get ready for my next communication, saying I would be doing a photograph reading. When I start a demonstration, I will usually ask people if they have brought a photograph with them – which many people do. The photographs are then collected and I put them onto a table on the stage. When it's time for me to do such a reading, I will go to the table, where I'll always be drawn to a particular photograph. From that photograph, I look to connect to a specific Spirit person.

Anyway, on the occasion in question I went to the table where all the photographs were laid out. As usual, I soon felt drawn to a particular photograph. I picked it up and showed it to the audience, so that I could determine who had brought this photograph to the event. The lady who had just been up on the stage with me put up her hand. 'That's Mam again,' she said. 'I asked her to show me a sign that she is here.'

I explained to her that I don't consciously pick the photographs – rather, I am drawn to them – and so this was her mother giving her the sign she had asked for. Then, with the photograph in hand, I said to the other sisters, 'I will try to reconnect with your mam at the end of the show and allow you all to feel her energy too.' They agreed and I continued with the rest of the evening's demonstration.

When the show was over, I asked the sisters if they would mind waiting for a while, as at the end of a demonstration I generally get a lot of people wanting to speak with me. Some will ask questions about how Spirit connects; others who didn't get a chance to speak during the show may want to tell me their own stories; others again may be those who had readings done and who want to thank me for making the connection with their loved ones. On this occasion, it took at least forty minutes for everyone to have a chance to talk with me and get whatever information or clarification they were looking for.

As soon as I could, I then went over to the family of

sisters and started to chat with them. All of them said they were delighted that their mother had come through and were very pleased with the evidence they had been given. Well, all were pleased except one – the lady who had verified the evidence, had come up and felt her mother's energy and had also received the sign she needed via her mother's picture. She made her feelings quite clear, saying, 'I wasn't too happy with Mam. She could have come through with more stuff for us.'

I stayed silent as she carried on, complaining that her mother hadn't said or done enough for her. After a while I said to her, 'Your mother came through with evidence that it was her, is that correct?'

'Yes,' she conceded.

'And your mother came through, singing some of the songs that she loved?'

'Yes, she did.'

'And you felt your mother's energy strongly when you came up onto the stage?'

'Yes, I did.'

'And your mother caused me to be drawn to her photograph just after I did the reading for you, didn't she – when you asked for another sign that she was here?'

'Yes, she did,' she said.

'And you are still not happy?' I said. 'Do you not realise the energy it takes for Spirit to come through so clearly, and in a room with so many people who are all looking for their loved ones to connect? Do you not think that other people would have loved the same things to have happened for them? What you have just said shows a complete disrespect for those in the Spirit World, and most importantly for your mother. I am appalled by your comments. Not for myself, but for your mother's sake, I am appalled.'

'Don't mind her,' one of the other sisters said.

'She's never happy,' said another.

And with that, the lady who had been complaining so bitterly started to make excuses, saying that I had misunderstood her meaning and that she was in fact happy that her mother had come through for her.

'Let's leave it at that,' I said and walked away. I was incensed at the comments she had made about her mother, who for about twenty minutes of the demonstration had come through so clearly and distinctly, with plenty of information that the family had been able to validate. She had even given the whole audience a good laugh at some of the things that she came through with and some of her quirky ways.

As mediums, we can only ever relay the information that the Spirit communicator gives to us, and I most definitely don't make up information to artificially enhance the experience of the sitter, nor do I embellish the detail that a communicator is giving. I give the information as I get it, whether the sitter understands the connection to them or otherwise.

Fortunately the type of situation I have just described has arisen very rarely for me. For that one bad experience, there have been any number of successful connections, when I have felt blessed at the powerful way in which those in the Spirit World have spoken through me, and I have been delighted to have been able to bring immense joy and comfort to those who have lost loved ones.

In terms of such positive experiences, I always think back to one occasion, when I was doing photograph readings at an event in the Civic Theatre in Tallaght. Funnily enough, this example also involved a group of sisters who were hoping to make a connection with their mother. As I looked at all the photos on the table in front of me, I felt drawn to a photograph of an older lady, so I picked it up and showed it to the audience. When I pick up a photograph, I will usually put it to my chest, so that I can feel the energy of the person in the photograph and draw them close to me, in order to better communicate with them. The lady in the audience who had brought the photograph put her hand up. I started to tell her that I had her mother with me. I was then able to say to her that she had come to the demonstration with five other people – which was correct, since her five sisters were there with her also. Her mother was so elegant in the way she came across to me, and I described her manner and appearance as very regal – 'Queen-Mother-like' is what I said. (When I describe a Spirit loved one's personality, I like to associate it with a personality that the sitter and other people in an audience can easily identify with.) The Spirit lady then came forward with some good evidence, some of which the family understood and some of which they said they recalled hearing before within the family, but would need to double-check after the show.

Once I had passed on everything their mother had given me, I asked who, out of the group of sisters, wanted to come onto the stage to experience their loved one's energy directly. It was decided that the eldest sister would come up. Nervously she walked down from her elevated position, four rows from the stage. (The auditorium in the Civic Theatre is tiered from ground level upwards, so everyone has a clear view of the stage area.) She then came onto the stage and sat on the sitter's chair.

'Are you okay?' I asked her.

'Yes,' she said. 'Just feeling a bit nervous – but looking forward to it too.'

I then asked her to close her eyes and allow her mind and her body to completely relax, explaining that the more relaxed she was, the easier it would be for her mother to enter her energy field and to connect with her. So she closed her eyes and took a deep breath.

I spoke to her mother's spirit, asking her to enter her daughter's physical body: 'Breathe the body, nice and easy – don't forget to breathe the body.' Next I said to the daughter in a low, calm voice, 'I am going to ask your mam to push her energy down into your fingers and hands, and then she will use that energy to move your fingers or hands, or to raise your hands – whichever she feels most comfortable with.'

I could see the sitter relaxing more and more, as her mother's energy got stronger and stronger within her body. With that, her left hand started to rise off her lap and there was a gasp of astonishment from the audience, as people whispered to one another, 'Do you see that? Look what's happening – her hand is lifting!'

I continued to speak with the mother, now telling her to keep pushing her energy forward, taking control of both of her daughter's hands if she wished. Very soon, the sitter's right hand started to move up off her lap in a flicking movement – as if she was thumbing a lift – and then quickly dropping down again. She kept repeating the same, very distinctive gesture. Then I asked her mother to place the hands back onto the lap and to relax her energy for a moment, after which she was to push all the way up towards her daughter's chest and neck, and give her a hug. 'You will feel a warm sensation in your heart area – then you will feel the sensation of a hug,' I told the sitter.

With that, she started to cry. 'I can feel Mam hugging me – it's tight, like she has her arms around my neck and chest – I can feel her, I can feel her!'

Finally I asked the mother to gently disconnect her energy from her daughter and to stand aside. The daughter opened her eyes, a huge, beaming smile on her face.

'You heard your mam talking to you as well, didn't you?' I asked her.

'How do you know that?' she replied.

'Because she told me you could hear her,' I said. 'This is not the first time you have heard your mother talking to you since she passed – but all the time, you have been doubting the fact.' The sitter nodded in agreement. As she stood up and went back to her seat, the audience applauded, amazed at what they had just witnessed.

'It is as simple as that,' I said. 'Just because we don't see our Spirit loved ones in the physical world, the way that we see each other, it doesn't mean we can't feel them just as close to us as they were when they were here, giving us a hug. We all can bring our Spirit loved ones that close to us again.'

At this, one of the other sisters took the microphone that was still in their row from earlier, when the eldest sister had been accepting the information I was conveying from their mother. 'Tom,' she said, 'I was a complete sceptic. Even with all of the information that you gave about our mother – things that you couldn't possibly have known – I was still a sceptic. I asked Mam if she was really there with my sister. Then I wanted her to do what she always used to do with her right hand. And she did it! Those movements we saw from my sister's right hand – that's exactly how she used to move her hand. That was her final sign to me, to say that she is really here with us.'

As she spoke, the sceptical sister began to cry, and the other sisters, who were already teary-eyed from having seen their sister experience the loving energy of their mother, broke down too, unable to contain the emotion any longer. A number of people in the audience began crying as well – these were not tears of sadness, however – they were crying with joy at having witnessed and felt the comfort, love and reassurance that these sisters had been able to receive from their mother who was now in the Spirit World.

~

I love to get feedback from people for whom I have done readings, as it is testament to the evidence that the Spirit World has given to me. It also greatly helps me in my growth and development as a medium, enabling me, for example, to keep building and refining my knowledge of how Spirit communicates with me in terms of references and symbols, and so on. It is very affirming to know, too, that I have been able to help people in an important way. Here are some examples of the type of feedback I have been very pleased to receive from clients:

> In my life, like a lot of people, I had frequented fortune-tellers, where I kept an open mind each time whilst having a reading done. As far as mediums are concerned, I had

never been to one and really had no clue what to expect or what their capabilities are. Around Christmas time in 2007, I made a booking to have a one-to-one reading with Tom. On the day my reading was scheduled, I found myself becoming extremely nervous and anxious. As fear set in as to what I might hear, part of me was contemplating cancelling my appointment. My father passed away suddenly in 2006 and a lot of questions had been left unanswered between Dad and I. Hence the reason I wanted to meet with a medium so much, and since then lots of people had suggested that I do so.

I had no expectations whatsoever before meeting Tom. Deep down, I secretly hoped he would recognise my father as being deceased, but not to the extreme of what followed. I truly was shocked and numbed by the things Tom came out with during my reading. These were things that only five people in this world could know – those being my immediate family.

My appointment for the reading was for 9 p.m. But it seems that my father had come to Tom that same evening at 8 p.m., providing him with his name (I still can't believe that). And then how Tom described my father during the reading was 100 per cent spot on for the person that he was. I never thought for one minute that Tom would say to me, 'Do you want to ask your father anything?' However, I went on to ask a couple of questions and truly felt such a calmness when doing so. This for me, I think, was the most unsettling (but amazing) feeling I ever experienced.

A week on, and I still find myself recapping all Tom spoke about. I tend to smile a lot when thinking about it. To sum up my reading, I feel so reassured to know now there is life after death, as this is something I did not believe at all up until last week.

~

My wife decided to book a reading after she had an experience at Christmas, when she felt that my father (who passed away many years ago) visited our house. She was very convinced, and insisted that he was here with us because something was going to happen and that we would find out soon what it was. I laughed at her at the time, because to be honest I just thought she was imagining things.

The next day my uncle died suddenly at the age of fifty-four. I was a bit freaked out by that because my wife had been so insistent, but life carried on and I let it go. When she initially went to see you with her own father, I laughed even more when she returned a bit disappointed because the reading hadn't worked out and you had asked her to come another night … She commented, however, on a number of things that you had said that were very validating for her, including the fact that she had experienced a visitation and that it wasn't all in her head. That was all she had really wanted to know.

I ended up at her second appointment by accident and if I'm honest, I was more than a bit sceptical. I expected that you would have to fish for information, or that you would say six or seven things and get one or two right. I was looking forward to teasing my wife about it afterwards! She was so convinced that my dad wanted to connect with us, and took his photo along to the reading.

On the night, I was totally amazed. In an hour and fifteen minutes, everything you said about my dad was spot on and extremely detailed. I was also taken aback, more than once, when you described situations in my childhood that only he and I knew about. It really was an amazing experience for me. I hadn't felt my father's presence since he died eighteen years ago, when I was still young. It was overwhelming to feel so connected to him again. It has also helped me to reframe my relationship with my father in some ways and connect with him man-to-man.

~

I attended a night in the Killashee Hotel, Naas. I was so taken aback as to what Tom could tell people. It was so comforting to all of the people who heard about their loved ones, from babies through to adults – it was very emotional. I didn't have a reading that night myself, but did have a one-to-one the next day. Tom used photos of two people I wished to connect with and, true to his word, he told me all the details I wanted to hear, right down to their names and things that meant a lot to me and one particular person who had passed. I would recommend attending a demonstration, as it is a wonderful and comforting experience.

~

I had gone to the show not knowing what to expect. It started slowly, but Tom got into it and things went from there. He said some amazing things and got lots of information – it was really accurate. My sister and I got details about family members who had passed, but couldn't give Tom any clarification at the time, as we were unsure about the details – but we got the information from family members and it was accurate.

~

My missus came back from the show and told me about what was said and the things Tom told her. I'm a bit of a sceptic, but those things can't be guessed and she was just so hyper, telling me all the stuff he said. It opened up something for her – made her smile, cry and remember things she'd forgotten. It just made her happy. If that's what it does, keep doing it, I say!

~

I received a very accurate reading from Tom last November. I had wanted to contact my sister for a long time, but had never been able to get the information I got from Tom. I brought along her ring but didn't say who I wanted to contact, and Tom was able to connect to her spirit through that.

It was amazing to watch, as I could tell he was hearing the information she was telling him. He told me that it was my sister who was with him and that she had died on life support. He kept pointing to his head, as she had bleeding on the brain. I was overwhelmed also, as he had picked up important dates and things about her personality too. He also received information that a baby boy was on the way and sure enough, a family member had a baby boy only two weeks later! At the end of the reading Tom let me feel my sister's energy. I just relaxed my arms by my sides and I felt a lovely warm, tingly sensation. I left on a high and was very emotional, as he said it was like there was an army trying to get through to me! I'm forever thankful to Tom, who gave me proof that my sister's spirit lives on.

I would like to finish this chapter with a true story in poetry form from Irene 'Durham' Simpson. Irene writes poems about her experiences with Spirit, and has kindly allowed me to include here this inspiring poem about a flower reading. A flower is just one of the many objects from which readings can be done, and, as in Irene's case, flowers can yield fascinating results.

Love of Plants

Our chairman said, 'Bring a flower next week,
As our Guest Medium reads them, we're told she's good.
From your flower, she can bring information you seek,
Of your Loved Ones in Spirit. So please if you could,
Bring a flower – along with your love.'
So as I passed by our family home,
I remembered our chairman's request.
I picked a rose from the garden my mother had grown.
A yellow one, for she'd loved those the best.
I took it with me – along with my love.
With my rose in her hand, that medium took,
Some minutes to study it, with a gentle touch.
Then in her eyes, came a faraway look.
'Your Mother is here! This rose says so much,
Mum's glad you brought it – along with your love.

These petals, with love are packed so tight.
Eight leaves represent the children she bore.
The last leaf dropped off. This one's with her in the Light.'
It's true! We were eight – the youngest is on Heaven's shore.
David's back with Mum and Dad – along with our love.
'Many roots, and long branches,' the medium claimed,
Spread out from my rose – giving a significant slant,
To the reading she gave, and to whom it was aimed.
For we are a large and widespread family called Plant!!
Till we all meet again – I send them my love.

Irene 'Durham' Simpson

10

EVOLVING WITH SPIRIT

> Perhaps they are not stars, but rather openings in heaven, where the love of our lost ones pours through and shines down upon us to let us know they are happy.
>
> *Eskimo Proverb*

In Chapter 6, we looked at ways in which any one of us can start to tune in to the Spirit World, heighten our awareness and take the first steps towards developing our mediumistic abilities. Learning to work with Spirit is an ongoing process, which can never be said to be complete, since there is always something new to take on board and there are always fresh ways in which you can grow and evolve. As I said earlier, any medium who tells you they know everything and have learned all there is to learn cannot in my view be embracing the Spirit World in its most complete sense.

If you have already embarked on the fascinating journey into mediumship – perhaps by attending a workshop, development circle or weekly class – or are still just considering it at the moment, there will be many challenges ahead, although constant challenge is what makes working with Spirit so exciting, of course. One of the most important pieces of advice I can give to someone wanting to get further involved in this area is that you should *take your time*. There are important responsibilities attached to the role of acting as a mediator between a sitter and a Spirit communicator – we will look at some of these in more detail a little later – and it's best to be aware of these before launching yourself into mediumship, all guns blazing.

It's never a good idea, for example, to rush into giving one-to-one readings on the strength of having done a weekend introductory course on mediumship. I have seen this happen, and it can be actively damaging for both the self-styled medium and their sitter(s). So, it's vital to allow yourself time to develop. In my own case, I didn't feel truly ready to give one-to-one readings for members of the general public until 2007, when I'd already completed a lot of training and been actively developing my connection with Spirit since the death of my Uncle Richard, back in 2001.

I mentioned earlier how a sitter can sometimes be struck by 'psychic amnesia' during a reading, and be unable to remember important facts about their Spirit loved one, often because of the sheer pressure they are putting themselves under in that moment to be fully responsive to everything. In the same way, when it comes to learning about mediumship, sometimes the biggest block to our development can be the strength of our own desire to make a connection happen. Connection to the Spirit World is never something that can be forced or *made* to happen – rather, it is something that can only take place when we relax, go with the flow and *allow* it to happen.

Very much related to this is something which I always tell people in my development circles and other classes – that above all you have to trust what you are getting from Spirit and never let your ego take over. This might sound easy, but it is sometimes the most difficult thing in the world to let go of our own ideas and thoughts about a situation, and our illusion of control over how things happen. Our sense of control over what Spirit decides to communicate is just that – an illusion. It is only once we give up our own perspective, and open ourselves up to all the other perspectives Spirit can bring, that true connection can really happen.

Some people in my development circles can experience almost the opposite problem when they first begin to receive communications from those in the Spirit World. Rather than jumping in feet first, they may feel very cautious about passing on Spirit messages to those they are intended for. Lurleen, who has been a very dedicated participant at many of my workshops, classes and circle sessions, as well as a regular attendee at our Spiritualist Union of Ireland church, recalls this feeling of hesitation whenever she first received a Spirit message for someone:

> I remember when I, a reluctant medium, had to pass on a message to another individual. It was while I was on one of my trips to the Sanctuary [the SUI church].
>
> On the bus that morning, I heard a young Spirit man give me his name and details of how he had passed. He wanted his friend, who was working at my house at the time, to know he was okay and also to tell his mum that she was not to worry – he was happy and safe. I asked the young man if he could come though again at the SUI service later, with a more experienced medium (me being the Doubting Thomas I was at the time).
>
> The young man obliged: he did come through again at the service that evening, with the same information he had given me earlier. When I got home the following day, I had

to figure out how I was going to tell his friend. A few days later I managed to find a way to tell him. He was surprised at how accurate the information was, but at the same time he was pleased to receive it.

One of the key things that all mediums need to look at is the *ethics* of mediumship. Lurleen's observations, and her experience of being 'a reluctant medium', tie in with an awareness of the important responsibilities which mediumship brings with it. As mediums, we must always keep in mind the fact that those who come to us looking to connect with Spirit are often going through the painful process of bereavement. (And, as anyone who has experienced it will know, this is a process that can never be said to be truly 'over' and does not have a definite time frame attached to it.) The person getting the reading is most likely already grieving over the loss of someone close to them, and going through the roller coaster of emotions and feelings which that entails – such as, for example, anger, sadness, pain, guilt, loneliness and abandonment. Over and above this, connecting with a loved one who has passed is in itself a deeply emotional experience. And so it is clear that a sitter's emotional state will be very highly charged and they will be feeling very vulnerable, so they must be treated with care. I truly believe that a medium can help with the process of bereavement by bringing healing and comfort to someone who has lost a loved one. But – as I said at the outset of this book and always make clear to my clients – visiting a medium is not a substitute for bereavement counselling: it is complementary to it.

I believe that the way in which I communicate with a sitter is crucial. By this, I don't mean changing the *information* you get from the Spirit communicator, to be able to tell the sitter what you think they might want to hear: I am referring to the actual *language* you use to convey the information you have been given. A medium, through the words he or she uses to express the information from the Spirit World, can play a very important role in lessening the anguish and pain of a sitter. This is especially the case with someone whose loved one has 'crossed themselves over' to the Spirit World.

My own view is that it doesn't matter the route that you take to return to Spirit. However, society does stigmatise different ways in which people return, particularly in the case of suicide. I find 'suicide' a harsh and pointed word with, as I have said, a sense of stigma attached to it. I prefer to acknowledge such circumstances by saying that someone has 'crossed themselves over' to the Spirit World. That person's spirit decided, before coming here to the physical world, how it wanted to leave again, once its sacred contract in this life had been fulfilled. Some people might say that this is in itself a harsh outlook on things – why would someone want to cross themselves over in such a way?

For the family who are left behind after someone crosses themselves over, society's attitudes to this manner of death can be very wounding. People will often say something to the effect of, 'Oh, there's that lady whose son killed himself last week,' or 'There's that lady whose brother committed suicide.' Very rarely will they say, 'Oh, there's that lady whose son died last week,' or 'There's that lady who lost her brother recently.' For the grieving family, there's a world of difference between these distinct ways of referring to the same event.

I am always aware that it's the very same when I am doing a reading for someone. I am very careful of the actual words that I use to describe how their loved one passed, which as we have seen is generally something which Spirit will show me when I connect. For example, let's stay with the lady who has lost her son through suicide. Let's say I have been able to connect with her son and he gives me the feeling and sensations that he was responsible for how he crossed to the Spirit World and that he passed through, say, a hanging. I could communicate the information he has given me in two different ways. I could either say to his mother, 'Your son gives me the feeling that he committed suicide and was found hanging from a tree, with his neck broken in three places.' Or I could say, 'Your son crossed himself over to the Spirit World through asphyxiation. I can see the tree beside which he was found. He is accepting responsibility for the way in which he passed.' In both statements, I am giving essentially the same information – but there is no doubt that the tone and brutal directness of the first will only add to the anguish, hurt and anger that the sitter will probably already be feeling.

This 'duty of care', which as I see it, a medium has to a sitter, means also that not only must you choose the words you use with care, but that sometimes you must be selective about the content of a message. Referring again to my example above, and the lady whose son passed by hanging, it is clear that it is sometimes in the interest of the sitter for a medium to withhold some of the more upsetting details of the circumstances of someone's passing – it would serve no purpose other than to increase this mother's anguish for her to be told that her son's spinal cord at the back of his neck was severed, and so on.

Another reason for caution in divulging every detail, especially when you first start out in mediumship work, is the consideration that your interpretation of what Spirit has communicated may not always be completely accurate. A good illustration of this is given here in a story from Marie, for whom, very interestingly, communication from those in the Spirit World often takes the form of dreams:

> I woke suddenly one morning. I looked at the digital clock, which said 10 a.m. exactly and could not believe the time, because I am never in bed at ten in the morning, unless I am unwell.
>
> I then remembered the dream from which I had just awoken. I dressed hurriedly – behind in my housework for the day, I needed to cover as much ground as quickly as I could.
>
> On coming down the stairs, I was very surprised to see my youngest daughter Mary enjoying a cup of tea in the kitchen, as she would never usually be up visiting me so early in the morning. The first thing I said to her was, 'You're pregnant', and she laughed so heartily you would think I had just told her the joke of the century!

To explain to her what my remark meant, I was forced to tell her about my dream – but not all of it!

I told Mary that I had dreamed I was in the waiting area of the hospital. To my left, there was a group of five men with their backs turned to me. They seemed to be chatting among themselves, though I could hear no sound. Although I never met my grandparents, as they had died before I was born, I had the distinct feeling that the man with the hat was my late father's father, bless them all. I knew they were all spirits anyway. To my right, there was a beautiful baby in a car seat, ready to go home. She was dressed in a white, all-in-one shell suit and wore a baby-pink baby beanie hat. The pink and the white were the only colours in the black and white scene in my dream.

I went over to the baby and said, 'Hello! You are a very beautiful baby. You are gorgeous.'

To my surprise, the baby spoke, replying, 'I am your new granddaughter, I am coming to Mary.'

I said, 'Oh! And you can talk!'

She replied, 'Yes, I can talk now, but not later', and we spoke some more, although when I woke up I couldn't remember what else we said to each other.

I decided not tell Mary about the spirits in the dream, however. In my mind, I had seen that the baby was ready to go home, but there had been no sign of Mary, so I thought the dream signified that Mary was going to die and I could say nothing. In fact, Mary had almost died of a clot in her lung after her second daughter was born and I was so afraid of a repeat performance this time that I now begged her to go to the doctor – she had been told that if she got pregnant again, she would need to inject herself each morning with a special anti-coagulant.

After much persuading on my part, Mary agreed to go to the doctor. He said that even if she were pregnant, it would probably not show up, as it was too soon. But she asked him to do the test anyway – no doubt, so that she would be able to go back to me and say, 'I told you so.' However, to her great surprise, her pregnancy was confirmed.

Sometime after this, Mary got a date in the post for a scan, as they needed to measure the baby to determine how much anti-coagulant she should take each day. So on the day in question, we both went to the hospital. While we were sitting down chatting, waiting for her to be called for the scan, I suddenly felt compelled to tell Mary about the spirits in my dream. To this day I have no idea why I felt I had to do this, but the feeling that I should tell her was so overpowering that I had to. She didn't seem to take much notice.

The nurse came to bring her down for the scan and they invited me to come also. But it was as if I was stuck to the chair in the waiting room – I could not move. I made an excuse and said I would be waiting there when she got back. Still, both Mary and the nurse were insisting that I come to see my new grandchild, but it seemed like I was glued to the chair, unable to move. Eventually they accepted that I wasn't going with them and went away.

About fifteen minutes later, Mary was back, hysterical from crying. Her beautiful baby had died – her little heart had not developed properly, and the scan showed both the reason and the time that the baby had died.

I had misinterpreted the dream – it was the baby who was ready to return home to Spirit, not Mary.

We knew the baby was a little girl: I had seen her baby-pink cap.

Mary called her 'Nevaeh' – 'heaven' spelled backwards, and she is buried with both of my parents.

In this dream state, Marie had been able to connect with her 'etheric record' and get a foresight of what was to come. This was not so much a Spirit communication, but an accessing of information about what was to come.

~

Another aspect of mediumship which requires time and patience, and which I focus on a lot with the people who attend my mediumship development circles, is *how to establish boundaries when working with Spirit.* This links in with questions I am frequently asked about how, as a medium, I manage my day-to-day life – people wonder if it isn't difficult to get through the list of daily tasks most of us have to get done, when I am receiving constant communications from Spirit. The key here, as with what I said above about the importance of how we word the message we have to pass on, is that you need to be in control of your mediumship, rather than the other way around.

It is true that when you first begin to connect with Spirit, it can often feel a bit overwhelming and all-consuming. Orla Shevlin, who was a committee member of the SUI, describes this well when she talks about the beginning of her journey into Spiritualism:

> We started to attend Tom's circle every week and [from there] our development was amazingly fast. Sometimes too fast – but all in a good way. Hearing Spirit, sensing its energy twenty-four hours a day, was almost overwhelming at times. Going to sleep was nearly impossible, as strange faces came so close to me I felt I could nearly [touch] them with my hands – all [were] wanting to connect with their loved ones. I needed to learn how to discipline myself, and also learn to rid myself of any doubts that might have been

> entering my head. But I just couldn't believe how well and how fast the information was coming.

Christine Noctor, who was also a committee member of the SUI and a working medium herself, recalls having the same kind of experience when she first began to develop her abilities:

> At first I was finding it hard to close down properly and had Spirit [people] visiting me all hours of the day and night. I was afraid to tell them to go away, as I was afraid they wouldn't come back. But as time went on, I found that they were only willing to speak to me [really effectively] when I was ready to listen.

My own early experiences were in many ways the same as Christine's and Orla's. Spirit knows no boundaries and doesn't make the distinction between day and night, or 3 p.m. and 3 a.m. – if we are ready to communicate, Spirit will respond in kind whatever the time and circumstances are. This can be overwhelming at times, or, at the very least, distracting and disorienting. So one of the things I work on with people in my development circles and classes is showing them how they can set boundaries with Spirit, and that they need not stay connected to the communication channels all the time.

Once limits have been set – along the lines of 'When I'm ready to connect, I'll connect, and when I'm not ready, you need to leave me alone, so that I can sleep, or focus my attention on the important day-to-day elements of my life' – Spirit will generally cooperate well. You need to be clear about what you need, however, and try not to give out mixed messages, which can happen when someone says they don't want to connect at a particular time, when all the while, at the back of their mind, they keep thinking about how much they would love to be in contact with a specific Spirit loved one there and then.

In some development circles these days, however, I think almost too much importance can sometimes be put on the protection of the self in mediumship work. If this is taken to the extreme, there is the risk that the connection to Spirit will close down at a certain point, since the person will no longer be sufficiently open and receptive to the communication process.

How much Spirit communication impinges on your everyday life can also depend on how mediumship works for the individual person. Because for me, Spirit messages are experienced mainly as part of my own thought processes, and don't involve any very unusual feelings or sensations, I find that I can drift in and out of a connection and link in fairly quickly to any information being given. I can do this in company, without those I am with realising what is happening – it's not as if I have to detach myself from what is going on around me and get down on my knees with my eyes closed, or anything like that, in order to be connected with Spirit!

Setting boundaries in this type of work is something which gets easier with practice, especially once you become more confident that doing so will not lead to Spirit shutting down altogether, never to reconnect. Each medium must discover for themselves what their own limits are, as Orla Shevlin explains when describing what works for her: 'I would try and meditate at least three times a week and also I [am] getting very disciplined with Spirit – I love my work, but it is very important to have "you time" and family time too.'

In looking at all of the issues above, it should not be forgotten, too, that working with Spirit can have its lighter moments as well: *Spirit has a sense of humour too.* Just as they may have enjoyed a laugh in this life, loved ones will generally retain a good sense of humour once they have passed to the Spirit World. I have experienced my own fair share of comical moments and encounters during my mediumship work. I always remember, for example, the time I was doing a house clearing (or Spirit rescue) at a property where the occupants had been experiencing a lot of troublesome Spirit activity. Not long after I arrived at the house, I was quickly able to make a Spirit connection. The spirit gave both myself and the tenants of the house, who were with me at the time, a great laugh when he told us about an occasion when the previous owners of the house had summoned a priest to the property to perform an exorcism, and he said that the priest had tried to drown him with the holy water! (By the way, the term 'exorcism' is little used these days, and is more likely to be referred to by priests or ministers of the orthodox churches as 'deliverance ministry'.)

On another occasion, I remember how at one of my development circles one evening, a member of the group began to channel a girl from inner city Dublin, who had passed from a drug overdose and was looking for her partner who was in the Spirit World – apparently, she didn't realise that she had already crossed herself. This spirit began to make fun of some of the people in the circle, which we all found very amusing. Then I asked her if she wanted to cross over to the Spirit World, and she said that yes, she did, and so I began to take the person who was channelling her through the process of Spirit rescue, to enable this Spirit girl to make the transition. When we had completed the process, everyone in the group began to attune to Spirit once more, to see if they could bring through any new connections. All at once, the same group member as before began to connect with Spirit as a 'channel' for communication again. When I asked her what she was getting this time, she replied with a direct communication from Spirit, which began, 'Hiya, I'm back!' With that, we all fell about laughing – it was the same Spirit girl from before: she had come back to tell us that she hadn't crossed properly! The laughing and joking went on for quite a while, until I finally asked her partner in Spirit if he would come forward and help her cross, which, to everyone's relief, he duly did.

While researching this book, I decided to ask a number of people – both those involved in mediumship development and those who aren't – whether they'd like to share any funny experiences they have had involving Spirit. Here are some of the replies I was given:

> My mum was just cleaning my son's bedroom for the first time since he had passed, when her phone, which was out

on the landing, decided to randomly ring me six times. Like most teenagers, my son never did have a clean bedroom, and didn't like people to be in his room. [I think this] was his way of saying 'Mammy, get her out of there!'

~

One Sunday night at home I was in one room and my husband in another. We heard the toilet seat bang (it's always down – he is well trained!). My husband popped his head round the door and said to me, 'What was that? I thought you were in the loo and that there was something wrong!'

A couple of minutes later, we heard the handwash dispenser activate. We went into the bathroom to find soap on the top of the surface near the sink. Lots of things happen [in our house] and it's always in the bathroom, which used to be a bedroom until we did a lot of renovation work. Anyway, that night, I just turned to my hubby and said, 'Well, at least they washed their hands after they'd been to the loo!'

~

Now, get ready for a laugh! [I was] conducting a lovely reading the other night, when the sensor of an air-freshener (which was very loud) went off. My sitter landed in my lap with the fright! It was so funny – and it kept happening. Spirit can have a very good sense of humour around me sometimes!

11

BLESSINGS IN DISGUISE – LURLEEN'S STORY

In Chapter 7, we looked at the spiritual journey of Rob Wright, my first 'student' in the world of mediumship. The story of Lurleen Drumm is another inspiring example of the potential we all have to develop our awareness of and our ability to connect with those in the Spirit World, regardless of the different backgrounds and life experiences each one of us may have had.

I first met Lurleen at one of my demonstrations in Donegal during my 'Feel the Spirit' tour around Ireland in 2009. I must say her determination in travelling from Donegal to Dublin on a regular basis – it is an eight-hour round trip from her home to Dublin – to come to evening classes, workshops and events at the Spiritualist Union of Ireland shows a huge commitment to her work with Spirit. Here, Lurleen recounts her spiritual journey in her own words:

Throughout my life, I have met with many difficult challenges or as I like to call them, 'blessings in disguise', but ten years ago a course of events would have a profound effect on me, bringing me on a soul-searching, spiritually awakening and deeply healing journey.

I'm a wife to a wonderful husband, Feargal, and a mother to three great children. I was born with cerebral palsy, which means that the right side of my body is partially paralysed or, to put it in my terms, I have a lazy right hand that doesn't always do what I want it to, and a weak right leg that has a tendency to fall asleep when the rest of me wants to get up and go! My philosophy in life has always been, 'What you don't have, you don't miss', as well as 'Everything happens for a reason' – it's just that we don't always know or understand why. But somewhere along the way, I believe, those reasons will always become clear.

Back in February 2006, my mum, Yvonne, was diagnosed with terminal lung cancer. It was just the last straw, after five incredibly difficult years during which my family had managed to overcome so much illness. My two sons, Jerry and Daniel (aged just two and a half and fourteen months at the time), had been diagnosed with childhood arthritis. Around the same time I had also been diagnosed with arthritis, and also four prolapsed discs in my back. This would force me to retire from a nineteen-year career caring for adults with intellectual disabilities. At this juncture, too, my husband Feargal had given up his job to return to full-time education to train as a nurse.

A few weeks after Mum's diagnosis, I started having very vivid dreams about my Nana Katie, who had passed on and who I was always very close to, as she had played a big part in my life. In these nightly dreams Nana Katie would sit on the edge of my bed, and it was all so real – I could feel and hear her, and even smell her Lifebuoy soap, which I remember she kept beside the kitchen sink when I was a child. In the dreams she would speak to me, saying: 'Lurleen, your mum will be with me for my anniversary. Please use this time to mend bridges with her.'

Mum and I had very similar personalities, which meant that we could often see the things in each other that we didn't like about ourselves. Although I loved her very much, I could never do anything right in her eyes. But as Mum's health deteriorated during that year, she became more dependent on me and, as a result, we became very close. Mum passed away on 24 September 2006 at 3 a.m., aged just fifty-eight. She was cremated two days later on 26 September, my Nana Katie's sixth anniversary.

After Mum's death, many strange things began to happen around the house. The lights in the kitchen would come on when the switch was off. (I suppose I wasn't surprised this happened in the kitchen, because Mum had been a chef all her life.) I would also hear her voice and smell her perfume – and even though I hated the smell of the stuff, it was a great comfort to me at this time! My daughter, Caoimhe, would also say that she could see her nanny sitting in her room at night.

At this time I was on strong painkilling medication for my back, and I wondered if this was what was causing me to hear these voices in my head. I felt I couldn't tell my husband Feargal, as he was by this time a psychiatric nurse and I was afraid he might think I was suffering from delusions! Instead, I asked Mum, Nana Katie, my Uncle Charlie, and my guardian angels if they could please send me someone who could help …

It took two years.

In October 2009 I came across an advertisement for a medium in my local newspaper: it was Tom Colton, and he was giving a demonstration in a nearby hotel the following weekend. Feargal wasn't working that weekend, so I asked him to go with me. I also asked him to go with an open mind.

The demonstration was brilliant. Tom enabled people to feel the Spirit presence of their loved ones, and I could clearly see what a comfort this was to those who had lost someone close. I realised why it had taken two years for my own angels and guides to answer my prayers – they were waiting to send me the right person! At the end of the demonstration, I arranged to have a one-to-one reading with Tom the following day. I was really looking forward to it, especially having spoken with him after the show.

The following morning I brought a photo of Mum with me to the reading. Tom was able to describe Mum's personality to a tee, and gave me other personal details that in my opinion he would have had no way of knowing. He then asked me if I would like to feel Mum's presence. As I could already feel her presence with us, I didn't feel the need for him to let me feel her and told him so, which was fine of course. When the reading was finished, I told Tom about some of the strange things that had been happening around the house since Mum had passed, and he told me about the workshops he was planning to run the following year. I said I would be interested and he promised to keep me posted.

On Valentine's weekend the following year, I attended the Sanctuary in Clondalkin, where Tom was hosting his first workshop in mediumship for that year. Before going, I had asked Mum for a sign that I was in the right place, the place I was meant to be. Near the end of the drive, as I turned the corner into the Sanctuary, I got the sign I had asked for: written on the wall was 'Kilcarbery Business Park'. I knew then that I was in the right place – my Nana Katie lived in a village called Kilcar on the west coast of Donegal, where I had spent many a happy day as a child.

The workshop was a brilliant experience. I met a lot of like-minded people, and Tom was a great teacher, very patient, and eager to show us how easy it can be to communicate with loved ones who have passed on. He kept telling us that you don't have to have any special 'gift' to be able to do this – all you need is faith and a willingness to open your heart and mind, so you can realise when those in Spirit World are communicating with you.

On the Sunday of that weekend of the course, I felt my paternal grandfather, Dan, come to me in a meditation we did with Tom. Dan spoke to me in Irish, which confused me. He also had my Nana Sinéad with him – she had only died three weeks previously. But I was puzzled about one thing: my granddad's first language was English, so why had he spoken to me in Irish? During the meditation I received the gift of blue scales from my grandparents (this was a symbolic gift passed on to me by my Spirit loved ones – other people there received such gifts as jewels and precious stones). I couldn't understand the meaning of the blue scales, and I began to doubt that it was my grandparents I was connecting with. I asked them if they could come through again at the service in the Sanctuary to be held that evening, where Tom would be demonstrating. Sure enough, that evening at the service, my granddad Dan came through to Tom, who was able to describe him so accurately that it was scary. Tom also gave a detailed description of my grandparents' holiday home in the Kerry Gaeltacht – which at last explained the earlier use of the Irish language.

As for the blue scales, this would not make sense until almost six months later, in June 2010, when Feargal and I bought an apartment from a solicitor and the interior was blue. (Scales of course are the symbol of justice and so were a symbolic reference to the profession of the previous owner of our new apartment!)

The second workshop I did with Tom was also exciting, and a fun-filled weekend for which our Spirit loved ones joined us. I particularly recall one of the exercises we did, where each of us had to tune into the Spirit loved ones of each individual in the group (it was decided in advance who we would all try to connect with). I remember fondly this exercise for two reasons: firstly, because I was given by Spirit a new symbol to describe a person's character – 'a hardboiled sweet with a soft centre'; and secondly because, when it came to my chosen person, my Uncle Charlie, everyone within the group was able to tell me something about him, including his date and month of birth. And even more surprisingly, when tuning into Charlie, Tom kept repeating the expression, 'Look at the pot, calling the kettle black'. I knew straight away what this meant. That very week I had undertaken to do something that my Uncle Charlie had also done twenty-five years previously, but for which I had questioned his motives at the time!

During that weekend, the term 'Doubting Thomas' also came up a few times for me. The first time was when I was doing Tom's meditation, 'Going Home – the Reunion'. In my 'gift box' – the one given to me by my Spirit loved one – I kept seeing a golden eagle. When I mentioned this to Tom afterwards, he suggested that the eagle could be one of my Spirit guides. I wasn't convinced, until the next time I did the meditation and opened my gift box to find inside the words 'Doubting Thomas' in big neon lights. What else could I do but laugh?

Today, as a member of the SUI (Spiritualist Union of Ireland), I try to go to as many as possible of the spiritual development classes and workshops in the Sanctuary. I also go to the Sunday services as often as I can, despite living four hours away. I have met some lovely people and made some great friends, with whom I keep in regular contact.

It never ceases to amaze me how my Spirit loved ones let me know they are around – like on a recent trip I made to Derry. On my journey home, the car in front of us had the letters 'SUI' (UI is Derry City's designated registration code) on its registration plate, as well as the numbers corresponding to the following day's date. Before spotting this, I hadn't decided whether I was going to make the eight-hour round trip to the Sanctuary the next day to go to its weekly service – but that number plate made my mind up for me!

It only goes to show, how, when you trust and believe, your Spirit loved ones can show you in the simplest of ways that they haven't really left at all. It's so comforting and inspiring to know this. As I continue along my journey, I'm still learning and growing from my experiences, as it's who I am.

Through mediumship and learning more about the Spirit World, I have found that I am honouring, nurturing and respecting Spirit. By so doing, I have enhanced all aspects of my life, and filled a void that lay deep within me. I have become more aware of who I am as a Spirit being and, by working with Spirit, for Spirit and through Spirit, I am respecting who I am. This is a very positive, enriching experience for me. Continuing to learn, grow and heal as a spiritual person has increased my sense of harmony and encouraged me to create a happier life both for me and the people who have chosen to spend this life with me: my family and friends.

We all have our roles to play, both within our own lives and in those of others – this is part of our soul's journey in unveiling itself and helping us remember who we really are. Through the help of my higher self and guides, both here and in the Spirit World, I have been able to continue to learn and grow spiritually.

The pioneers of Spiritualism have taught us that we too can become pioneers for future generations, and also that life continues after death, on a plane of higher consciousness and in another dimension within the universe. This inner knowledge has changed my whole understanding and perception of Spirit, and how I feel, hear and see it. I feel more complete as a person and am truly grateful to have been able to embark on this inner journey towards discovering who I am as a Spirit being.

Lurleen Drumm

12

BUILD IT AND THEY WILL COME

> Therefore, if personality exists after what we call death, it is reasonable to conclude that those who left the earth would like to communicate with those they have left here.
>
> *Thomas Edison*

On 24 May 2009 the Sanctuary, Ireland's first Spiritualist church, opened its doors to the public. This initiative had come about after I and six people from my Celbridge development circle – Olive Grogan, Anne Redmond, Robert Wright, Dolores Malone, Tracey Kane and James Molloy – along with Declan Flynn (whom we met on the trip) had spent a week at the Arthur Findlay College in Stansted in April that year. During our time there all of us had been struck by the fact that, with over 400 Spiritualist churches around the UK where they could develop and practise their skills, the British mediums we had met were spoilt for choice, whereas for us Irish mediums there was not a single such place to go to. So, together, we decided that it was high time that the Republic of Ireland had its first Spiritualist church!

We were very much aware, of course, that any new religious groups trying to establish a presence in Ireland have always been met with huge suspicion and resistance. We each knew that if we were to try to get a Spiritualist church up and running, it would take a lot of hard work and dedication from all of us. But our excitement and enthusiasm at the thought of having such a spiritual hub in Ireland for like-minded people meant that we were able to embrace the thought of the challenges which lay ahead and made us even more determined to make it happen.

Over the weeks that followed we had many discussions about what our next steps should be in setting up the church. We quickly put together a committee, with a president, vice-president, secretary, treasurer, events and PR manager, and so on. Each person was allocated a specific set of responsibilities and various practical tasks, including the huge job of researching all the necessary legal issues that we knew needed to be taken into consideration. As well as some of us from the core group, a few people who were not part of the original Celbridge circle were keen to join the committee. Not only were we all extremely motivated, but as a group, we also managed to work together highly effectively – so much so that, within just four weeks of our return from the course in Stansted, the Spiritualist Union of Ireland was born.

Our mission was clearly stated from the outset: the aim of the SUI was to 'Work with Spirit, for Spirit and through Spirit'. This is the backbone and essence of what the union is all about. Otherwise, we tried to keep the number of rules and regulations to a minimum, as none of us – especially myself – likes red tape. I've always felt that to be truly effective, it's best to keep things as simple as possible.

Another key decision we took was that we would refer to our new church as a 'Sanctuary'. We all felt that this was a far more fitting word for our purpose, knowing that, particularly in Ireland, as soon as you mention the word 'church', if you are not affiliated to any of the established, mainstream religious groups, the immediate conclusion people will jump to is that your organisation must be a cult.

Predictably we met with a lot of resistance and mistrust as soon as we went public with the founding of the SUI. I remember doing an early radio interview for BBC Radio Ulster about Spiritualist weddings, which we were intending to offer as part of our new set-up, along with other religious Spiritualist ceremonies. The presenter asked me a lot of questions about the weddings and what the Spiritualist ceremony would entail, and I was happy to answer in as much detail as I could. Next, however, the presenter told me they had a minister from one of the Protestant churches on the line and that he wanted to talk to me live on air. This gentleman started off in a fairly composed fashion, telling me that in his church they also believe that the human spirit lives on after physical death. But then he said abruptly, with sombre meaning, that this was the only common point between his belief system and mine: that this was where any similarity ended! He went on to tell me in no uncertain terms that I was doing 'the work of the Devil', and that I should ask the Lord Jesus Christ to come into my life to save me from myself, and so on and so forth.

Remaining calm, I explained to him that that was his belief system – he believed in the Bible and what it says – and, while I didn't share his beliefs, I certainly respected them. I said that all I was asking from him was the same respect for my belief system in return. If I was Jewish, I put it to him, would he still try to press his views on me and say that my religion was 'the work of the Devil'? 'I think not,' I said in conclusion. He seemed a little lost for words at this.

But it wasn't over just yet. The radio station then decided to bring some of their listeners into the conversation, asking people to call in with any questions they might have for me. The first caller was also an advocate of a Protestant church, and this conversation went pretty much the same as the last one, with this man telling me that I needed to bring the Lord Jesus Christ into my life if I was to have any hope of eternal life – and that, he was sure, Jesus would forgive me. The next listener to come on the line started in a very similar way and ended up delivering the same lecture as the others.

Wouldn't this world be a wonderful place if people respected each other's opinions, even when they didn't necessarily agree with them? If each of us was able to just accept another person's point of view and belief system without trying to take them apart? There would certainly be less war and far more peace in the world.

Of course I wasn't surprised to come up against this type of reaction to the setting up of the Spiritualist Union and the Sanctuary. And naturally it wasn't just those belonging to the Protestant churches who voiced their disapproval: we were – and sometimes still are – met with suspicion and resistance from the different religious groups across the board. People's perception of what a Spiritualist is differs vastly – but there is still a lot of ignorance about our belief system in society these days, and a surprising number of people today still see what we do as akin to dabbling in the 'dark arts' and the occult, and so on. Clearly, this is not the world I am involved in at all, as you can tell from reading this book.

A quick look at the history of Spiritualism clarifies a number of things even further. The belief in, and the practice of, communication with spirits has existed in all nations throughout human history, and certainly predates modern religion. In ancient times primitive man had no doubt that his ancestors survived death, and in fact ancestor worship was a form of religion. And spiritual phenomena have occurred throughout human history, with people being entranced, inspired and influenced by Spirit intelligences. During moments of ecstasy, in dreams, reveries, drug-induced states and deep meditations, people have experienced Spirit awareness. In fact, mankind's history, literature, folklore and fairytales are full of mystical spiritual beings, both good and bad. The Greeks consulted oracles, and the Egyptians and Romans practised fortune-telling and prophecy to obtain guidance from the gods. Even today, some cultures still have their witch-doctors and shamans, who invoke the powers of Spirit for healing and guidance.

In terms of Christianity, there are many examples throughout the Bible of spiritual happenings: divinely inspired speeches and messages, speaking in tongues, the hearing of voices, angel messengers foretelling the coming of prophets, and so on. One of the best-known biblical instances of communication with the Spirit World relates to the Witch of Endor (also known as 'the medium of Endor'), who, according to the Scriptures, raised the spirit of the deceased prophet Samuel, so that the Hebrew king, Saul, would have the opportunity to question his former mentor about an upcoming battle (see the First Book of Samuel, Chapter 28, Verses 5–23, in the Old Testament). There are many other key episodes in the Old Testament which relate to mortals receiving divine communications: in the Book of Exodus, Moses goes to the summit of Mount Sinai to receive God's instruction on the Ten

Commandments; also in Exodus, there is the incident of the Burning Bush, where we are told that an angel of God appears in the bush to tell Moses that he should lead the Israelites out of Egypt; in the book of Genesis, Abraham is 'told' by God to sacrifice his son, Isaac, but the angel of God intervenes at the last moment to save the boy's life.

Later, in the New Testament, we are told how the founding of the Christian church relied heavily on Spirit communication and other phenomena that could be described as mediumship. We are told that, after Christ's death and resurrection, the apostles receive direct inspiration from the Holy Spirit, which will compel them to spread the news of Christ's story and preach his Word:

> And when the day of Pentecost was fully come, they were all with one accord in one place. And suddenly there came a sound from heaven as of a rushing mighty wind, and it filled all the house where they were sitting. And there appeared unto them cloven tongues like as of fire, and it sat upon each of them. And they were all filled with the Holy Ghost …
>
> *(Acts 2:1–4: King James Version)*

In the fifteenth century, however, Christian leaders

decided that the use of psychic and mediumship abilities was wrong, unless exercised exclusively by the Christian priesthood. All others who possessed and practised such spiritual powers were denounced by the church as 'false prophets', evil sorcerers, witches or heretics, who were liable for severe punishment – and for centuries this attitude held powerful sway.

In 1484 the pope strongly denounced mediums, and, in 1486, sanctioned the publication of a book entitled *Malleus Maleficarum* (or 'Hammer of the Witches') that reiterated the belief that all those who communicated with spirits were witches and should be severely penalised. There followed centuries of persecution, where people suspected of using psychic abilities were in danger of trial, torture and execution. During these times, thousands of mediums were put to death by church-sanctioned 'witch-hunters'.

Spiritualism did not emerge from this dark period of oppression until the eighteenth century, when figures such as the eminent Swedish scientist and astronomer Emanuel Swedenborg became renowned for philosophical writings that were, he said, inspired by Spirit teachers.

It was not until the middle of the following century that Spiritualism began to come to the fore as a widely recognised system of belief. This happened first on a broad scale in the US, where a famous incident that took place in Hydesville, New York State, in 1848 brought the whole issue of mediumship and Spirit communication to the attention of the general public.

On 31 March that year, having been troubled in their family home for some months by a series of rapping noises and other audible disturbances with no apparent explanation, two young sisters, Margaretta and Catherine Fox, established intelligent, two-way communication with a Spirit person, who was apparently responsible for producing the phenomena. A committee of investigation was formed and also managed to make a connection with the Spirit person who had been harassing the Fox family. It was a Charles Rosna, who had been murdered and buried beneath the cellar of the Fox family's homestead. An excavation of the cellar later proved that there were indeed the remains of a body buried there. The publicity that these events aroused and the investigations carried out at the time led to mediumship being discussed openly and to huge public interest in the whole area of Spiritualism.

That day in March 1848 is now widely credited by many as the date of the beginning of the modern

Spiritualist movement. Within just a few years many groups of Spiritualists had formed in America, with the aims of seeking psychic phenomena and considering the religious implications that lay behind the teachings received from Spirit. In time, both the phenomena and the teachings attracted the attention of eminent scientists and intellectuals in America and beyond. A Mrs Hayden brought the new knowledge to England and openly demonstrated mediumship there. She was persecuted and insulted by the press and by some in the established Christian church, but her mediumship was defended by public figures, such as Welsh social reformer Robert Owen. Owen went on to embrace Spiritualism, having witnessed Mrs Hayden conducting successful Spirit communications.

In 1853 the first Spiritualist church was established in Britain at Keighley in Yorkshire, and the first Spiritualist newspaper, the *Yorkshire Spiritual Telegraph*, was published in 1855. By the 1870s there were numerous Spiritualist societies and churches throughout the country, many of which still survive.

Today, Spiritualism allows all people to witness, and establish for themselves, communication with the Spirit World. Whereas in the past, society at large condemned such practices as dangerous and evil, in recent years particularly, much of the ignorance and fear concerning Spiritualism and the Spirit World itself is melting away, and everyone can benefit from the love, guidance and wisdom from those who have gone before us into the realm of Spirit.

So, I suppose when you consider what those involved in Spiritualism in the past had to go through in terms of public persecution, being at the receiving end of a few sermons from devout Protestants on a radio chat show isn't so bad after all!

By the middle of May 2009, our preparations for the grand opening of the SUI Sanctuary were well on track. It still amazes me that we were able to get so much accomplished within the four short weeks between our return from the Arthur Findlay College and the day of the official opening. Each of us had worked hard and played our part. Robert Wright created an excellent emblem for the SUI and the Sanctuary. I had found what I thought would be suitable premises for us and, luckily, when I took everyone to view the property they immediately saw the possibility of it becoming a good home for the SUI. Everything we needed to get the SUI operational was paid for with donations/membership fees. We had all of the initial paperwork completed and filed with the various bodies and authorities.

As opening day approached we were rushing frantically to get all of the final practical things sorted out. We realised, for example, that we would need to source a large number of chairs for the opening ceremony – at least 120 in order to fill the room. Our budget was fairly limited as you can imagine, and so the best bet seemed to be to search the Internet for a good deal on this number of chairs. Eventually I came across a college that was selling 120 chairs from one of their computer rooms. I rang the contact number as soon as I could, explaining to the lady who answered that since we were just setting up and had very little money, we would really like to be able to pay in instalments. Fortunately she agreed that it would be possible to pay over a period of three months. An artist, James Deane, painted beautiful murals on the walls.

Now that we had our chairs and everything else in place, we were finally there – the first Spiritualist church in the Republic of Ireland was ready to open its doors to those who wanted to embrace Spiritualism! On 24 May 2009 the Spiritualist Union of Ireland was launched. We were full to capacity: every seat was taken and there were people standing all along the back of the room. About

130 people in all gathered in the Sanctuary to witness the first public service. This was a very proud and moving day indeed for all of us.

Robert Wright was and is a great events manager and, with everyone's input, had come up with a great programme for our opening ceremony. Whilst in Stansted, Robert had met with a number of mediums from all over the UK, and with their help and cooperation he was able to put together an initial database of mediums and inspirational speakers, some of whom came to participate in our opening event. These people also provided a great deal of support and knowledge to us generally in the setting up of the SUI, which was invaluable and gave us a fantastic platform to start from – and we are truly indebted to all of them.

The opening ceremony and the various demonstrations that were part of it went off brilliantly, and we were all delighted. It seemed we had really been able to reach out to a lot of people who were looking for this kind of spiritual centre. All the work that had gone into organising and setting up the SUI and the Sanctuary was worth it!

Today the Sanctuary continues to hold services every Sunday. It is open to all members of the public to attend, free of charge, to get messages from loved ones in the Spirit World. We have evening classes and weekend workshops on all aspects of spirituality as well as mediumship development circles, retreats and other related events. Everyone is welcome to come along to all of these. (For more information, please see our website, www.spiritualistunion.com.)

At our Spiritualist services, a portion of the time is generally spent on a demonstration of mediumship, where a medium will link in to the Spirit World to communicate with Spirit loved ones on behalf of those present. Often a guest speaker will also give an address looking at elements of personal and spiritual development, general spirituality, mediumship, spiritual healing and spiritual enlightenment. Generally there is a musical element to the service too.

The purpose of the Spiritualist Union of Ireland is to promote Spiritualism in Ireland and facilitate both the general personal and spiritual development of its members, particularly in the areas of mediumship, spiritual healing and all other aspects of holistic and spiritual enlightenment. Whenever challenges and dilemmas arise in the running of our organisation and the Sanctuary, which of course often happens, we always come back to our core principles, and the answers are there for us: *Working for Spirit, with Spirit, through Spirit.*

13

OVER TO YOU!

During the writing of this book, I decided to review some of the most frequently asked questions people put to me about the Spirit World and mediumship. I consulted my archives of correspondence, and also asked people in my development circles and classes what questions they had puzzled over themselves when they first started on this path. Here is a selection of the type of key questions, which I will try to answer as best I can, by drawing on the insight, experience and information I have built up over the years.

My eleven-year-old daughter saw her grandfather in the corner of her bedroom last week. She said he smiled and waved at her, and that he looked the same as when he was alive. She closed her eyes and when she opened them, he was gone. I feel it was really him but don't know much about spirits appearing. What was happening?

It is very common for our Spirit loved ones to make appearances in our lives, to let us know they are around and that their spirits live on after physical death. Some people see them, some hear them and some people feel or sense their presence. Encourage your daughter to keep an open mind about Spirit, and tell her that it is nothing to be afraid of: her grandfather and other Spirit loved ones are just there to help her on her journey. Her grandfather may even be one of her guides – the Spirit entities who are chosen by us and for us before we come here, to help us in this life.

How do we build a closer bond with our Spirit guide(s)?
Taking time to meditate and attune to the Spirit World will help our connection to our guides. Sometimes we stand in their way, but they only want to help us, so we need to trust in the process and just hand over to them and allow them to help when the time is right. They are always there, ready to connect with us, even though sometimes we forget this or don't feel their presence. Most of the time, we just have to open up to our Spirit guides and this in itself will forge a closer bond with them. We also need to give them permission to connect and to give us guidance. They cannot interfere in your

life path, but they can support and help you along the way.

Do you think people who do very wrong on this earth have a lot to do by way of penance when they pass over? Do they go to a different level to others?

My belief around this is that we are all part of a bigger picture and bigger plan, and sometimes we don't see this or understand where we fit into it all. When someone who has done things that are regarded as wrongs by society crosses to the Spirit World, they go to the exact same places as everyone else.

We are made up of two primary elements: our physical body and our Spirit body. One helpful way to explain how this works is by using the analogy of a car and a driver. The car is our physical body, and the driver is our Spirit body. The directions on the satnav are our sacred contract. So we set our satnav according to our contract, and the car follows the scheduled route. The Spirit body helps steer the car along the route, but must at all times follow the route. So the journey of an individual is predetermined in this sense. So, if someone's satnav has them down as a person who will do wrong to others, then this is what will happen.

But, looking at this from a different perspective, for every hard lesson or perceived wrong, there is an opposite, positive effect. For example, if the Second World War hadn't happened, then the parameters by which war crimes are policed would not have been established. Many, many wars have happened in the past, but there was no proper regulation of how people who had wronged others were dealt with. Now there is, with the War Crimes Tribunal in The Hague.

When someone does wrong in the present, we don't always see the positive outcome or what the future may bring. And some people are so blinded by a perceived wrong that they will never see the possible positive outcomes that it may also have.

When I raised this issue with Spirit this message came through to me:

> What would the world be like without colour? The grass would not be green; the sky would not be blue; the sun would not be yellow. What if everyone looked the same, felt the same and lived life in the same way? As each colour is different, so is each one of us different also. We all bring a unique aspect to the picture of life. If we were all the same, the world would have no emotion, no hue and no character.

> We must respect each other and our colours. Whatever colour a person is, is right for them. We shouldn't try and change them, but respect them for what they are.

If our contract says that we will change our ways then we will. Everything is in divine and perfect order. Sometimes we may never know why some terrible things happen, but I truly believe they happen for a reason.

My thirteen-year-old daughter sees Spirit, as I did as a teenager (and sometimes still do). How do I go about helping her develop this ability? She passes on messages to her friends and their families, but I don't know what to do to help her. She tells me that she wants to embrace this fully.

It is great that your daughter wants to embrace Spirit, and that you are encouraging her to do so. Allow her to develop her abilities in her own time, and don't force or push her in this regard. Check your local area to see if there is a Spiritualist church that will allow your daughter sit in circle. Some churches will allow this, with your permission and supervision. It would be great for her development to have the opportunity to sit in circle and experience the Spirit World in a supported environment.

Do you think souls that have passed on with unresolved issues with loved ones on this earth come back, or can't move over to the other side until they connect with these loved ones and attempt to address the issues in question? Is it only then they can pass over?

This question can have a multitude of answers, as each case is not straightforward and all can have different outcomes. When they pass, some people feel that they cannot cross over to the Spirit World, so they come back again to be around their loved ones and hence will remain earthbound. They may be there to support and guide their loved ones during the various stages of bereavement. Then, when they feel it is okay to go, or if their loved ones give them 'permission' to detach from them – and by that, I don't mean forget them or disregard them – then they can finally cross to the Spirit World. Once this happens, they realise that they can still visit loved ones from the Spirit World and that they don't need to stay earthbound in order to do this. An issue they may have had with a loved one when they were still alive will have been part of the contract that they signed up to, as valuable lessons for both parties will have come from this relationship.

Exactly when a spirit ultimately crosses over is a matter for each individual: there is no 'ready reckoner' for when the transition to the Spirit World happens. From the times I have performed or overseen Spirit rescues in circle, I can say that it often seems that a spirit has been brought to or guided in the direction of a circle or an individual that can help them make the transition to the Spirit World. Sometimes, spirits may feel that if they cross over into the veil of the Spirit World (i.e. no longer remain earthbound) they may not be able to return to be around their loved ones.

My belief is that when spirits cross over, they will reflect on what they have done in this life. Perhaps the conclusion will be that they should have been a better father or a better mother or a better friend – but had they not been the way they were when on the physical plane, valuable lessons may not have been learned by their loved ones here. Everything in our lives happens for a reason and, although we may not find this easy to accept at the time, these things – such as difficult relationships – help to shape and mould each of us into the people we are now.

When a person feels like something is going to happen and it does, and this seems to happen frequently, would this be classed as intuition, or something else?

Knowing that something is going to happen, or sensing that we have experienced something before, is an instance of connecting with our etheric records, or sacred contract, and tapping into information we already have knowledge of. This information comes into the conscious mind from the 'soul star', which is just above our heads, where our sacred contract is held – and we get it as it happens, or just before it happens. The information is familiar to us because we will already have included it in the map of our lives, before coming to the earth plane.

The plan of each of our lives is an intricate one. In this sense, life can be compared to a busy train station. We are the trains and our contracts are our timetables. Each train is set to be in the station, sometimes at different times and sometimes at the same time as other trains; we stop at many platforms – some repeatedly, some never again.

Have you ever reached, or got close to, the point where you thought of giving up working with Spirit?

That is a really interesting question. I think that when our lives are most challenging to us, we will often in turn challenge our Spirit guides, along the lines of, 'Well if you are here, I need you to do X, Y and Z for me!' When you don't feel you are getting the answers you want from the Spirit World, then you may begin to believe that it is not there or not important, and begin to question why you are working for Spirit at all, since you don't seem to be getting any assistance or guidance. But of course that is not necessarily the case – Spirit and our guides are there to support and help us, not to live our lives for us, or make the decisions or choices that we don't want to make for ourselves. We always need to remember that, ultimately, we have decided what happens in our lives.

So, yes, I think that sometimes we all reach a point where we say we have had enough and want to abandon the struggle. But the truth is that Spirit never gives up working with us – our guides never go away; they are always there. We are the ones that sometimes block them out or lose the connection with them, but they and Spirit are never too far away.

I have been told that when your time is up you are welcomed by your loved ones. I do hope so. Will my lovely mum be there to meet me?

Yes, this is true. In all the readings that I have done, Spirit loved ones have come through and acknowledged the different people that were there to greet them as they crossed over to the Spirit World. It is also interesting to note that very often, before someone passes, they become more aware of Spirit around them – they may for example start saying that they see their mother or father or sister or aunt – or someone else close to them who has already crossed over to the Spirit World. They may start talking to these loved ones, or begin to recount memories associated with them, and so on.

Our Spirit loved ones are there to support and guide us as we make the transition. Sometimes however, it can happen that the person crossing cannot see them – perhaps because they have passed suddenly and it is a big shock to them, something they don't understand: this is what some earthbound spirits have fallen into. They may not want to cross over; they may want to stay around loved ones still on the earth plane. But yes our loved ones are there when we cross. And sometimes it can be the ones we least expect to be there who will be waiting to help us.

In relation to this question, I would like to cite a piece written for this book by Melissa Bruce from Australia. Melissa is very connected to Spirit and has been working on developing her mediumship abilities for a number of years. Melissa's testimony of what she witnessed at the moment of death of her husband's beloved grandfather is very moving, and evocative of the essence of Spirit:

I have seen Spirit in many forms for most of my life, but never has it been more beautiful or so close than after the passing of a dearly loved one …

Just recently my husband's grandfather fell sick with cancer, again. At eighty-three years old, we knew this man's time with us was limited. For my husband, his grandfather was the most important person in the world: the man who taught him everything. We made as many visits as we could to see him, sit with him, talk with him, and say what we wanted to say.

We were there at the moment he passed, and for me it was a privilege to be able to watch the greatest gathering of people in the Spirit World I had ever seen, as they came together to welcome this wonderful man home. One by one, his parents, relatives, close family and friends all gathered together, in anticipation of his arrival. Knowing that no one else around me could see this beautiful sight, I watched as they all assembled around him.

The moment he passed, it was like I was seeing a whole new man – young, handsome, able to build an entire house by himself if need be. I watched him plant a kiss on the top of my husband's grieving head – just as my husband had done to him on our previous visit.

At the funeral, he was also there. I could see him and I could see the love and the tears he had in his eyes, as he looked at his wife of sixty-five years, his children, grandchildren and great-grandchildren – all gathered there together because of the love we had for him and the love we all knew he had for us.

I have never seen such a beautiful transition before, from the family I had seen gathering to greet him, to my own connection with him, so strong – it was a very powerful and emotional experience, and one that I don't think I will ever forget. My husband and I now have a new, very powerful ally in the Spirit World, a part of our great army. And all this time, both of us can still feel the love this man has for us, even if he has left us in the physical form.

EPILOGUE

We never stop learning. We go through our physical lives constantly learning new things. Even in the Spirit World, when we return there, we learn new things based on our experience and continue to learn. To empower ourselves with new knowledge helps us raise our awareness, raise our consciousness and raise our understanding. We all have the knowledge we need within us and it is released from our higher self when we are ready to receive and embrace it.

In life we may feel isolated, on our own, not connected to anyone. We feel surrounded by people we cannot relate to, cannot connect with and cannot feel comfortable around. But with those in the Spirit World, you never feel isolated, or alone, or as if you don't fit in. Spirit understands you, regardless of how you look, how you feel, what you believe. *We are Spirit, Spirit is us.*

Death is Nothing at All

Death is nothing at all.
I have only slipped away into the next room.

I am I and you are you.
Whatever we were to each other,
That we still are.
Call me by my old familiar name.
Speak to me in the easy way
which you always used.
Put no difference in your tone.
Wear no forced air of solemnity or sorrow.
Laugh as we always laughed
at the little jokes we enjoyed together.
Play, smile, think of me. Pray for me.
Let my name be ever the household word
that it always was.
Let it be spoken without effect.
Without the trace of a shadow on it.
Life means all that it ever meant.
It is the same that it ever was.
There is absolutely unbroken continuity.
Why should I be out of mind
because I am out of sight?
I am waiting for you.
For an interval.
Somewhere very near.
Just around the corner.
All is well.

Canon Henry Scott Holland (1847–1918)

MERCIER PRESS
IRISH PUBLISHER - IRISH STORY